WHAT PEOPLE ARE SAYING ABOUT TRIPLE BOTTOM-LINE COMPLIANCE

The concepts and examples in Triple Bottom-Line Compliance *are relevant across many areas of compliance, and illustrate broad applicability of the principle that good compliance, enabled by strong employee engagement, is good for business.*
LESLEY TRAVER, VP OF QUALITY AND COMPLIANCE, JOHNSON & JOHNSON

Compliance professionals face unprecedented challenges, and this book is critical in helping them develop the business acumen, perspective, and approach they need to be successful today.
JASMIN SETHI, FINANCIAL SERVICES INSIDER AND FORMER SEC SPECIAL COUNSEL

Triple Bottom-Line Compliance *provides a thoughtful, conceptual framework as well as practical guidance and case studies for compliance professionals. Whether you're at an early stage of your career or have years of experience, you will benefit from the original ideas and reminders for addressing the daily challenges of your demanding but rewarding job.*
DONALD KAPLAN, FORMER HEAD OF US COMPLIANCE, METLIFE

Practical advice that both challenges and inspires. Beth gives compliance professionals a refreshing view of their value.
CHAD ESLINGER, CCO, VOYA INSURANCE AND ANNUITY COMPANY

The crucial handbook for any compliance officer who wants to make more of an impact.
MARYJEAN BONADONNA, CCO, AXA ADVISERS

In almost every chapter, Beth shows us that when compliance and business leaders partner, clients and shareholders win. She then gives us a pragmatic roadmap on how to make that partnership a reality.
MATT PISANELLI, T. ROWE PRICE

TRIPLE BOTTOM-LINE
COMPLIANCE

TRIPLE BOTTOM-LINE
COMPLIANCE

HOW TO DELIVER
PROTECTION, PRODUCTIVITY,
AND IMPACT

BETH HADDOCK

Published by Advantage, Charleston, South Carolina.
Member of Advantage Media Group.

ADVANTAGE is a registered trademark, and the Advantage colophon is a trademark of Advantage Media Group, Inc.

Printed in the United States of America.

10 9 8 7 6 5 4 3 2 1

ISBN: 978-1-59932-945-1
LCCN: 2018933436

Cover and layout design by Carly Blake.

This publication is designed to provide accurate and authoritative information in regard to the subject matter covered. It is sold with the understanding that the publisher is not engaged in rendering legal, accounting, or other professional services. If legal advice or other expert assistance is required, the services of a competent professional person should be sought.

Advantage Media Group is proud to be a part of the Tree Neutral® program. Tree Neutral offsets the number of trees consumed in the production and printing of this book by taking proactive steps such as planting trees in direct proportion to the number of trees used to print books. To learn more about Tree Neutral, please visit **www.treeneutral.com**.

Advantage Media Group is a publisher of business, self-improvement, and professional development books and online learning. We help entrepreneurs, business leaders, and professionals share their Stories, Passion, and Knowledge to help others Learn & Grow. Do you have a manuscript or book idea that you would like us to consider for publishing? Please visit **advantagefamily.com** or call **1.866.775.1696**.

To all those who have taught me lessons—my mentors, peers, students, beautiful family, and yoga teachers! With gratitude and in that spirit, I share lessons with my readers.

TABLE OF CONTENTS

FOREWORD

We live in an era of major transitions—in the climate, in technology, in demographics, and in geopolitics—that are disrupting the way we live our lives, manage our businesses, and invest our wealth. The pace of change in these interconnected forces is unsettling many traditional beliefs and leading to a polarization of opinion on how to tackle the major challenges that confront us. The Global Financial Crisis of 2008 still lingers at the forefront of our collective consciousness, with a clear memory that unbridled market forces do not always allocate resources efficiently or responsibly.

The global economy and stock markets have regained much of their former health, yet there is a recognition that the maximization of short-term gains is no automatic panacea for creating a sustainable, inclusive, and resilient system. A generational shift is also underway with a growing realization that long-term prosperity is inextricably linked to the health of the planet. Sustainability, therefore, is no longer seen as an option, but increasingly as an imperative by companies and investors alike. Both recognize that a more sustainable approach to the management and deployment of capital doesn't just preserve the quality of life on the planet, it also leads to more sustainable and resilient financial returns.

Rapidly changing technology, regulations, and consumer preferences are combining to create the potential for stranded assets in a wide range of industries, as well as for the emergence of entirely new high-growth business segments. For senior executives, this poses severe challenges for which many are ill equipped when plotting the strategic direction of their managed firms. Boards can no longer rely on "business as usual" to see them through, and are often insufficiently diverse in thought and experience to recognize the extent of the unfolding changes.

There's no easy solution to the challenge for business leaders on how to assimilate these forces into the successful and sustainable development of their firms—with standard, historic management behaviors undermined by a world of disruptive and unsettling change. Yet expectations continue to rise for the integrity of company executives and their ability to evidence that they are taking seriously their responsibility to all stakeholders, not just the most vocal shareholders. Innovation and strong governance have become unlikely bedfellows. Investment firms also face these same challenges, with traditional risk models and modes of analysis being increasingly undermined by rapid changes in the factors influencing market and company behavior. Technology offers news ways of analyzing and then trading a myriad of data points at lightning speed, though often at variance with the capital allocation horizon of the companies in which they invest, challenging the claim of managers to be "long-term investors."

Asset management firms collectively look after tens of trillions of dollars of client assets, which brings enormous responsibility to not only invest this wisely, but also to recognize their obligations to the wider economy and planet. As the beneficiaries behind these assets begin to find their voice and express their preference for how and where their wealth should be used, asset managers will need to offer high levels of transparency to demonstrate alignment with the values of their customers. Good stewardship of those assets will become paramount and managers will be increasingly called to account for their actions, including how they vote on behalf of their beneficiaries and how they constructively engage with the companies in whose stock their clients' wealth is invested. It is no surprise, then, that regulation of financial services is no longer about adherence to rules, but about how organizations conduct themselves.

Triple Bottom Line Compliance is a timely book. It addresses the importance of strong frameworks of governance to enable the creation of successful businesses in a changing world, businesses that recognize the complex array of positive and negative impacts they have on the world—and how to manage these—to become more resilient, productive, and sustainable. Companies impact nearly every geographic region of the world and every sector of human activity, bringing an unprecedented ability to deliver better outcomes for many while developing new markets. The asset management industry—as a conduit of capital between savers and commerce—is also in a powerful position to influence behaviors through where and how they allocate the wealth of their beneficiaries and how they engage with the companies in which they invest. To ensure their effectiveness in delivering on these strategic opportunities, organizations must integrate the right values across their businesses, which is where sustainable governance steps in.

The important message of the book is that strong compliance creates the right culture for businesses to thrive and adapt in a world in transition. It ensures that the ethical values of an organization are not only consistently implemented, but are also integrated at every level of the business, and are reinforced by education, leading to higher efficiency and long-term value creation. Financial returns and corporate responsibility are the twin pillars of modern business thinking, and adding the third pillar of sustainable governance ensures enduring protection, productivity, and impact.

Building a successful sustainable governance culture is not easy, yet it brings enormous economic and cultural impacts for the long-term benefit of any organization. *Triple Bottom Line Compliance* will guide compliance officers on how they can successfully help their companies manage their way through an ever-changing world without losing sight of their financial objectives and broader responsibilities.

Andrew Parry
Head of Sustainable Investing
Hermes Investment Management

ACKNOWLEDGMENTS

This book could not be written without the inspiration and support of the compliance officers and others who helped on the journey toward sustainable governance. A special thank you to Andrew Siegel, Vaughn Swartz, Lisa Crossley, Dennis Kelleher, Mary Toumpas, Beth Shanker, Larry Block, Heather Traeger, Brian Rubin, Janine Diljohn, Jaynthi Gandhi, Andrew Parry, Howard Goldberg, and Kat Olin.

INTRODUCTION

CHANGING THE IMPACT
OF COMPLIANCE

This book is for compliance officers who want to make more of an impact within their organizations and profession. It shares strategies for delivering a new type of compliance system that not only defends and protects an organization, but also proactively helps it perform better. Compliance officers who commit to the system will be rewarded personally and professionally, enjoying more influence, camaraderie, and a sustainable contribution.

Collectively, compliance officers protect our economy by increasing market transparency and guarding customer interests. Individually, they can stabilize, propel, or even enable the downfall of the organization that employs them.

What power! Yet compliance officers face a host of issues limiting their influence. There is a narrow perception of the value of Compliance to an organization (I'll use a capital C for Compliance programs) and a misunderstanding of the inherent conflicts of interest compliance officers wrestle with daily. This leads to debates about the cost of Compliance and complaints about bureaucracy. Compliance officers learn—too often on the job—a great deal about the drivers of business interests, behavioral incentives, and the importance of relationships. Compliance officers need to know the rules, but their knowledge and technical skills can only take them so far if they simply pay passing attention to developing business acumen and the ability to influence and make sound judgment calls.

This book addresses why compliance officers in the trenches need not only technical expertise but also a business system. It changes the conversation about Compliance and presents a system of how to deliver **sustainable governance instead of bare compliance**. It shows the reader how sustainable governance can produce a better return on investment (ROI) for Compliance resources and increase brand protection, risk mitigation, productivity, and employee engagement. To that end, this book is addressed to current and prospective compliance officers and the people who work with them. The compliance officer role is rewarding, but inevitably leads to sensitive, and sometimes difficult, situations. You'll read candid and inspirational stories of lessons learned and why it's time for a sea of change in Compliance. My colleagues and I are sharing our insights in hopes that other compliance officers can make more of an impact, and in turn, pass along their own stories to others. Let's change the impact of Compliance from technical fundamentals to a competitive advantage—one compliance officer at a time.

I didn't always plan on becoming a compliance officer and governance attorney when I was growing up in the New York City suburbs, with a school principal for a father and nurse practitioner for a mother. As I grew older, though, I became inspired and guided by my grandfather and his career as a public servant, assistant district attorney, and judge to pursue a career in law. Thus, I moved to Washington, DC, where I lived and worked for ten years. It was on Capitol Hill as a legislative analyst—and later as a plaintiff class action attorney—that

I started thinking about the best ways to build governance programs.

As a litigator, I was able to see what companies were doing wrong. From there, I decided to go in-house as an ethics officer, working inside companies to help them incentivize responsible behavior and avoid liabilities and lawsuits. The first company I joined, Acacia Financial, provided life insurance and socially responsible mutual funds. From there I moved on to AXA Financial, a global financial service company. After almost ten years there, I became chief compliance officer (CCO) at the international firm Brown Brothers Harriman & Co. I was involved in building a Compliance program at a time when new rules were transforming corporate governance. My work at Brown Brothers Harriman provided a wonderful opportunity to also handle governance, Compliance, and legal issues in Europe and Asia. Then I returned to a US-registered investment adviser, Guggenheim Investments, where I helped build an infrastructure and Compliance culture.

After attending an executive program at Yale University, I started my own consulting business, Warburton Advisers, where I specialize in coaching Compliance leaders and helping companies to build Sustainable Governance programs.

I work with companies in financial services and the emerging field of FinTech, which is innovating the finance industry with more modern technology. This book will explain the importance of that technology and behavioral economics while borrowing from the megatrend, environmental, social, and governance (ESG) investing, in which Sustainable Governance programs are encouraged and valued.

I believe in the power of contribution and enabling others, whether senior management, boards, compliance officers, or students. I have served on a nonprofit board for the Brooklyn Music School for years, and have worked as an adjunct professor because I love mentoring. I am also part of the Impact Collaborative, a consulting group that helps many organizations, including technology companies, schools, and nonprofits, with social responsibility and governance.

Organizations have long recognized that they need a gatekeeper to be accountable for regulators, handling the technical requirements of compliance. But that gatekeeper role has grown and become more complex and difficult in recent years as business has become more global, more automated, and continues to rapidly innovate. The compliance officer can and should be a senior leader at the table for decisions to be able to give counsel at the right moment. A compliance officer is not just protecting the organization and mitigating regulatory risk as a gatekeeper, but is also helping the organization realize its full value—whether it's measured in profitability, growth, stability, credibility, or fulfillment of its mission.

Organizations have three incentives to build a Compliance program: avoiding liability or prosecution, adhering to legal or regulatory requirements, and meeting the need to set expectations for ethical conduct and shared values. Furthermore, a Compliance program shows investors, consumers, potential recruits, or donors that the organization is well run. So, a Compliance program can be used like an insurance policy (against liability or prosecution), it can be treated as a requirement, or it can be leveraged as a business differentiator. When an organization leverages its Compliance program as a competitive advantage, that fuels its ability to truly impact culture and results, changing the way we look at its cost and value.

This book offers eight strategies as a system to transform compliance foundations into a Sustainable Governance program that also makes an economic and cultural impact. Compliance officers can be so focused on technical requirements and risk management that they fail to deploy the soft skills they need to become influencers. The Triple Bottom-Line Compliance System offers a path for compliance officers to master the inherent conflict of the role, build credibility as trusted advisors, and protect their and the organization's reputation using business acumen instead of scare tactics.

THE SYSTEM INVOLVES EIGHT STRATEGIES. EACH STRATEGY WILL HAVE ITS OWN CHAPTER IN THIS BOOK:

1. Aligning

2. Verifying

3. Serving your client

4. Networking

5. Building legal alliances

6. Mastering diplomacy

7. Being your true north

8. Branding yourself and contributing

Stories offered to illustrate the strategies are composites of different experiences or are fictional. The stories are being told to make a point, not to cover all the facts, laws, and options involved. Opinions expressed in this book by me and other experts I quote should not be taken as legal advice for actions or decisions that may be required in similar circumstances and are personal opinions that may not represent their employers. Some colleagues who spoke with me to share their experiences asked to remain anonymous.

I hope you'll use what you learn in this book to influence your organization. You'll use it for your personal brand and for your own development, but please pay it forward as best you can: train others, start discussion circles, or pass along the book to a new compliance officer. Compliance officers are given great responsibility and authority, and are often thrust into sensitive situations, which they can handle better if they have mastered these strategies.

Before laying out my eight strategies in chapters 2 through 9, I'll begin with a big-picture overview in chapter 1 of why a focus on technical compliance is outdated and compliance officers must adopt the new Sustainable Governance approach.

CHAPTER 1

WHY IT'S TIME FOR THE
END OF COMPLIANCE

An affable senior manager at an investment firm is talking on the phone with a pharmaceutical expert about his drug company's clinical trial. The expert, relaxing in his home office, starts to talk about something else he is passionate about—helping people with Alzheimer's disease. He talks about his disappointment that a drug his team spent years working on will be denied government approval. The manager excitedly gets off the call and places a trade betting that the stock of the pharmaceutical company that produced the drug will decrease when the negative news is announced. He makes a lot of money for the firm and himself because his bonus is based on the profitability of his trades.

In this scenario, the firm is exposed to liability for trading on Material Non-Public Information (MNPI). Let's assume Compliance receives a regulatory inquiry about insider trading and must decide how to respond.

If Compliance is oriented toward regulatory enforcement risk only, here's what could happen next:

- After an investigation in collaboration with attorneys and others, the senior manager is disciplined, most likely fired.

- All proceeds of the trade are donated to charity so that neither the firm nor the manager benefits.

- Compliance informs the pharmaceutical company that its employee shared MNPI if appropriate.

- The compliance officer resolves the matter with regulators and discloses the outcome to any affected clients, the firm's board, and others, as necessary.

The Sustainable Governance approach includes the above—protecting the firm from regulatory risk—and then goes further. Compliance adds value that will prevent another employee from making the same mistake by changing the very drivers that enabled the insider trading. How this happens will be covered in depth in chapters 3 through 6, but some examples are:

- A new video training program is launched covering the harm caused and lessons learned from this scenario. Employees are reminded about the company's policies against insider trading.

- Compliance works with management and human resources to develop compensation and performance incentives promoting good business judgment. Employees are rewarded for self-reporting and collaborating on Compliance initiatives. They are downgraded for failure to support Compliance efforts and adhere to protocols, and for poor business judgment and ethics. Compliance helps the business identify high-potential leaders and consider department performance bonuses instead of individual rewards for profitable trades.

- The firm augments operational controls to detect insider trading by building a report on profitable trades that follow a call with industry experts. Managers can use the same reports to review productivity and performance of the investment team.

- The firm reassesses its compliance policies and controls for allowing such calls. The industry expert might be required to certify that he will not disclose MNPI. The calls might be recorded or include "compliance chaperones."

- The firm prohibits discussions altogether with certain companies or sectors if surveillance is too cumbersome to increase the productivity of business leaders and compliance efforts.

TECHNOLOGY INNOVATIONS

Technology is providing ever-changing ways for Compliance to rapidly discover issues before the regulators do or before the issues have systemic implications. The specific methods are beyond the scope of this book, but it is increasingly common for Compliance in financial services to use data mining for trading trends, which could be a sign of MNPI, or same-day reversals, which could be evidence of buying or selling equities to hide operational mistakes or insider trading.

When we talk about delivering triple bottom-line Compliance and the end of bare Compliance focused on protection only, we are applying lessons learned through behavioral economics.[1] Understanding behavioral drivers and incentivizing behavior is more effective than dictating rules and expecting adherence because Compliance publishes an edict. Compliance officers who rely on quick fixes spend their days firefighting. Sustainable Governance takes a longer-term approach, changing the way people work together by aligning interests and relying on incentives to win wider engagement that helps avoid problems. Sustainable Governance develops its own momentum so a compliance officer can almost step back and only calibrate improvements as needed.

In the Sustainable Governance approach, management and Compliance are accountable for maintaining incentives and continually educating people in the organization about expected norms and values. Those at the top lead by example and set the culture. People are respected, rewarded, and promoted within the organization for good judgment and ethical behavior. An organization lacking such incentives creates moral hazards unintentionally because Compliance is consumed with firefighting.

It is difficult for compliance officers to excel at their job. The laws, rules, and regulations are voluminous. If a compliance officer works in an organization where management has not bought into the idea of Sustainable Governance, Compliance is not included in strategic initiatives until the last minute when there is not enough time to study the impact of the issues or educate employees to avoid

---

1   References to behavioral economics draw on research conducted at the MIT Sloan School of Management and published in a 2006 article by Nina Mazar and Dan Ariely that is cited in the resources section at the end of this book.

missteps. Compliance is an afterthought instead of being embedded in the business process. As you will read in chapters 3 through 7, Sustainable Governance requires compliance officers to have the business skills of project management, strategic planning, and time management. They must be diplomatic and have strong relationships within the organization and their industry.

When an executive seeks guidance from a compliance officer and says, "I need it in a half-hour," the compliance officer who has broken out of the firefighting cycle says, "Thank you for reaching out to me. I understand the urgency. Is this a hard deadline? Can you tell me why we have only thirty minutes?" Based on the answer, the compliance officer can propose a reasonable time for responding to the request.

The compliance officer who is committed to Sustainable Governance can deliver Triple Bottom-Line Compliance: protection, productivity, and impact.

The protection comes from the compliance officer's technical knowledge and independence. Today's influential compliance officers are not technical bureaucrats handling approval forms and monitoring processes; they are focused on discovering and mitigating regulatory, legal, operational, and other risks by creating protective systems.

The productivity results from programs that are not just reactive quick fixes but are geared toward promoting efficiencies and incentivizing good judgment and behavior. Compliance officers bring value by implementing governance controls that build on or improve existing workflows, minimizing bureaucracy and additional costs. When issues are detected and addressed with sustainable solutions, the organization is more efficient and measurably more productive.

The impact is ensuring that Compliance is not merely a cost center, but also adds sustainable value that translates into better financial returns. Effective governance is powerful—it can increase brand credibility and employee engagement and lead to a culture of social responsibility and better product development. At the bottom line, scandals are costly, especially when an institution such as a bank that relies on public trust is exposed for wrongdoing. With environmental, social, and governance (ESG) and impact investing, we see many examples of the link between stellar governance and increased shareholder value. Public companies such as L'Oréal and Unilever have shown that when leaders align organizational values and incentives with governance, they make an impact more widely than just producing profit for shareholders at any cost. They create a sought-after brand and corporate culture that attracts loyal customers and differentiates them when recruiting and retaining top talent, including high-potential millennials.

STATUS QUO COMPLIANCE

TRIPLE BOTTOM-LINE COMPLIANCE

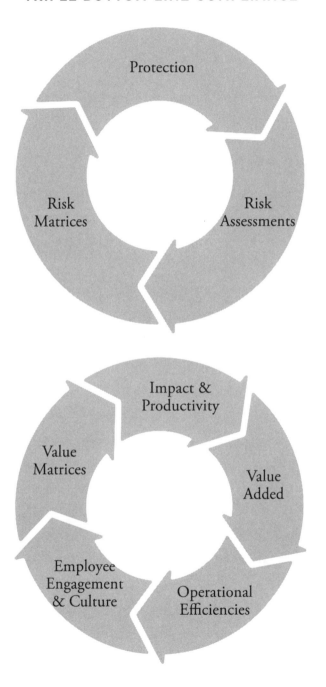

With a Sustainable Governance approach, compliance officers can tie Compliance expenditures to business value, just as they tie regulatory requirements and risks.

Compliance officers can inventory value added such as:

- new products

- new distribution channels

- new clients

- innovative process improvements

- efficient remediation of control gaps to incentivize good business judgment, ethical behavioral, and sustainable solutions that prevent repeated mistakes and errors

CONSIDER THE ALTERNATIVE

In the absence of Sustainable Governance, product development and distribution occur without contemplating behavioral incentives and governance controls. Time and money may be wasted marketing new products if a compliance officer is brought in too late to address issues. The product is already baked, so Compliance fixes are more likely to be bolted on instead of baked in. Product developers may not focus on avoiding conflicts of interest, self-dealing, and unfair expense allocations. SEC enforcement cases have been filed against firms for selling products that were designed with excessive costs and inappropriate expenses. Some examples are cases about:

- failing to offer investors the most appropriate or least-expensive share class of a mutual fund

- charging an all-inclusive monthly fee for brokerage accounts that are not trading frequently enough to justify it

- improperly allocating management expenses to private fund investors

Triple Bottom-Line Compliance is based on evolving trends in corporate responsibility, behavioral economics, and technology, but it's also based on conventional wisdom. Compliance officers should engage and influence others to be effective. They should deputize the employees in the organization in which they work. At times, the business thinks Compliance is too bureaucratic, the lawyers think Compliance is not analytical enough, and regulators think compliance officers are co-conspirators. If compliance officers want to make an impact, they must have a strategy. Knowing the rules isn't enough.

There are inherent conflicts of interest in having regulatory duties as a gatekeeper and employment duties as a client-centric leader. To reflect the dual reporting, this book will use the blended term "Glients" for those served by compliance officers.

The time is ripe for a Sustainable Governance approach for three more compelling reasons:

- The US government has begun prosecuting compliance officers for what regulators perceive as poor or negligent performance within their organizations.[2] That's an alarming trend because both the employer and the government evaluate a compliance officer's performance, but with the government, the compliance officer lacks the benefit of performance feedback or protection of employment laws and may be prosecuted despite best intentions. Sustainable Governance efforts to incentivize ethical behavior can be cited as a defense to such negligence claims.

- Increasingly, technologies such as artificial intelligence, robotics, and data analytics are being used in regulatory audits. Organizations must employ the same level of sophistication, which can't be implemented if Compliance is too busy firefighting. (See the resources section at the end of the book for a supporting study by the McKinsey Global Institute.)

- There is an increasing demand for ESG investments from major institutional investors, such as pension funds. They

---

2   Luis A. Aguilar, "The Role of Chief Compliance Officers Must be Supported," US Securities and Exchange Commission, last modified June 29, 2015, https://www.sec.gov/news/statement/supporting-role-of-chief-compliance-officers.html.

often seek to align their investments with sustainable development goals (SDGs) and the United Nations-supported Principles for Responsible Investment (PRI). (See Resources for an online explanation of PRI.) Demand to adopt the PRI mission continues to grow, with more than eighteen hundred companies around the world committed to promoting investment in sustainable and responsible organizations. As demand increases for impact and ESG investments, so too will expectations for Compliance to operate a Sustainable Governance system.

Building a sustainable and responsible culture is so valued to protect customers and investors; some government regulators outside the US require that pension funds invest in ESG or impact investments. In the US, the California Public Employees' Retirement System (CalPERS) is investing hundreds of billions with that same double bottom-line focus—driven by financial returns and responsible corporate behavior. I have built on that double bottom-line concept a step further in saying **Compliance can also leverage its efforts to protect an organization, to deliver a Triple Bottom Line.**

What's involved in building a Triple Bottom-Line Compliance department? The organization's leaders must commit to the concept, set the tone, and spend the money on basic costs, such as staffing and technology. But the competitive advantage of Sustainable Governance means that the organization avoids costly mistakes and gains brand credibility and trust.

MAKING OR FAKING
ESG CERTIFICATION?

Sarah Canter, the compliance officer for a global investment firm, has wrapped up year-end work and is eagerly planning next year's training program when a call from the head of the Berlin office, Christian Helm, interrupts the early morning calm. He sternly explains that a client at a large pension fund requires a complete description and report on the firm's ESG investing strategies. The client is seeking a certification that its funds have been tracking those guidelines from the time of the initial investment.

"Why are you calling Compliance? I don't make the investment decisions. Talk to the investment team," Sarah says reflexively. Christian is insistent, and senior in the organization, and the compliance officer realizes that passing the buck is not the way to manage the situation. A better response would have been offering to be a liaison between Mr. Helm and the investment team. "What if the investment team doesn't have proper guidelines and hasn't been investing in the manner the German pension fund expected?" she wonders.

Realizing the risk of a false certification, Sarah decides to work with the investment team to make sure that what is given to that German client is accurate, comprehensive, and transparent. She gets details from the Berlin office about when the client came on board, what promises were made, and what communication occurred. If there were any compliance gaps, she will make sure the investment team knows how to respond.

Compliance officers must maintain independence and not

get involved in investment decisions, but must also not pass the buck and miss an opportunity to uncover and address any governance problems. There may be some inconsistency in the investments because of a lack of written protocols. Or maybe the investments were perfectly consistent with the client's expectations, but the documentation was inadequate or just didn't reach the right people. Regardless, the compliance officer can add value by improving the system.

CHAPTER 1 TAKEAWAY

As a compliance officer, if you work in a culture of Sustainable Governance you can advance your personal brand and career development. It's important to become a change agent or avoid an organization that doesn't understand a compliance officer's strategic role in the success of the organization's bottom line. A compliance officer focused on governance comes off more as a leader who understands his or her impact on the rest of the organization. Instead of just thinking about technical requirements, answering the questions asked, or putting out the latest fire, the successful compliance officer is improving productivity, processes, and performance. The next chapter offers a strategy for aligning with an organization's culture or serving as a change agent for Sustainable Governance.

CHAPTER 2

ALIGNING THE MISSION
FOR SUSTAINABLE GOVERNANCE

ark Temple has been working in Compliance in financial
services for several years and knows he has the leadership
ability and temperament to be a chief compliance officer
(CCO). He has been making discreet inquiries within his network, so he
isn't surprised when he gets a call inviting him to interview for a compli-
ance officer position at a small but prestigious firm in New York. Excited
that the firm's famously well-connected CEO has reached out to him
on social media, Mark is eager to interview with this highly respected
financial services leader. The CCO position is newly created, the CEO
says, and Mark would report directly to him. Mark quickly reads up on
the firm on its public website, meets with the CEO, is ecstatic about the
generous salary offer, and accepts the job the next day.

What's wrong with this story? Mark didn't meet with anyone at
the firm other than his new boss. He didn't do any research to find out
whether the firm was financially stable or had regulatory problems.
Mark jumped at what seemed to be a lucrative opportunity without
asking the right questions. As a result, he could have joined a firm
with pending regulatory investigations and a command-type culture

that could make it impossible for him to be the kind of independent, ethical leader a firm needs to navigate through compliance issues.

Mark's story is fictional, but the idea that a CEO could maintain high stature in the financial services industry while perpetuating fraud is real. Bernie Madoff was the former chairman of NASDAQ when he was arrested and imprisoned as one of the biggest fraudsters in recent times. He had many employees who went to work for years unknowingly participating in a Ponzi scheme. His sons, one of whom was his compliance officer, eventually turned him in after years of reaping the benefits. Bernard L. Madoff Investment Securities was a peculiar Wall Street outlier, but companies do have a wide range of cultures.

This chapter discusses how to understand the culture of your organization or prospective employer and use it to your advantage. A compliance officer can be held accountable for failure to prevent others' bad conduct, so **it's important for Compliance and its mission to be aligned with the organization's culture and its leaders.** We'll look at how to tell if an organization has an infrastructure that helps it to not only mitigate risk but also incentivize engagement and collaboration. Whether you are building on an existing culture of responsibility or serving as a change agent to prevent scandal, you need to do two things: (1) understand and leverage behavioral economics, and (2) understand the drivers of your organization.

*"Tell me and I forget, teach me and
I may remember, involve me and I learn."*

—BENJAMIN FRANKLIN

A compliance officer needs to influence employees and management's behavior to deliver Triple Bottom-Line Compliance. Behavioral economics starts with understanding the incentives that will drive a desired outcome—in a compliance officer's case, that would be engaged employees who use good business judgment and ethics. A compliance officer can use behavioral economics to first build trust with employees. Trust will lead to loyalty and, ultimately, engagement. These factors cascade like a waterfall that lands on the Triple Bottom Line: protection from regulatory enforcement risk, increased productivity, and impact. If the waterfall is strong and consistent, then Sustainable Governance is the result. Bureaucracy and distractions are minimized. Employees are collaborative and engaged in self-reporting, and the organization has strong brand credibility, avoiding scandals that are often "predictable surprises"—crises that could or should have been foreseen—known to employees who are disinterested in helping build a responsible culture.

Thinking about this image of behavioral economics can help compliance officers assess an organization's drivers and culture (see box on the following page.) Traditionally, compliance has been based on economic theories that assume employees tend to act rationally in their own business interests and are motivated by money. Studies of that traditional approach indicate that only about one-third of employees care about their work. The rest—the disinterested employees—are more likely to perceive compliance as a bureaucratic distraction and are less likely to engage in reporting or fixing known compliance gaps. With the engagement of employees, compliance officers can do more because employees are aligned and help build the governance structure. Upcoming chapters will explain how compliance officers can give rewards, recognition, and incentives to increase buy-in and collaboration.

A report published in April 2017 by the Incentive Research Foundation titled "How to Effectively Harness Behavioral Economics to Drive Employee Performance and Engagement" highlights how the behavioral economics approach capitalizes on the power of emotions in increasing employee performance and engagement. An excerpt:

"Behavioral economics recognizes that 70 percent of human decision-making is emotional as opposed to rational. So it proves to be a more useful tool than traditional economics in helping employers understand what actually motivates employees ... Intrinsic rewards increase the recipient's self-esteem by establishing or affirming a sense of purpose, fueling a desire to live up to expectations of peers and social norms, or helping the recipient master new skills. Intrinsic values create a long-lasting desire to perform well."

An organization must prioritize and value business ethics, compliance, and employee engagement for these behavioral economic incentives to work. They won't work when efforts aren't authentic, and a Compliance program is window dressing and ultimately bureaucratic. Compliance officers should look for signs that an organization is not committed to developing an aligned and engaged workforce, or for signs that senior management is exempt from ethical standards.

Compliance officers may need to lead the cultural shift and influence the tone at the top—the board, executives, and managers—so the tone is aligned with behavioral economic practices that have been proven to work. New compliance officers generally hit the ground running and should aim to understand the situation they face within the first ninety days. In an organization that is less transparent, this may take more time.

"Bureaucracy is based on a willingness to either pass the buck or spend it."

—ANONYMOUS

In the story at the beginning of this chapter, a compliance officer neglected due diligence at a crucial time—when finding a new job. Asking the right questions before taking a job in Compliance is necessary to make sure there's a good fit on three tiers: (1) the organization, (2) the potential manager or boss, and (3) the other business leaders within the organization. Ideally, all three tiers are dedicated to Sustainable Governance and believe it will lead to more investment, more clients, more profits, and a better work environment. Our fictional "Mark Temple" talked to the boss but didn't research the organization, meet the other business leaders, or ask basic due diligence questions. A compliance officer, as a gatekeeper for regulators, is vulnerable to personal liability—and potentially even government prosecution—for bad conduct anywhere in the organization. Therefore, a compliance officer must be confident that he or she is aligned with the company's culture before taking a role, or else be prepared to manage through adversity.

SOME ADVICE FOR JOB-SEEKING COMPLIANCE OFFICERS

Before committing to a job, make sure you are aligned with the organization and its leaders. Don't just advocate for yourself as a candidate. Complete due diligence as you would before you buy a house or decide to marry. Your choice of employer will impact your contribution as a compliance officer. You could have extraordinary knowledge and communications skills, but still not add value if you are a cultural misfit. A misfit struggles to make headway and build rapport, and may not feel confident enough to persevere through adversity.

Voices of Experience

Throughout this book, colleagues of the author offer their experiences and advice:

MARY TOUMPAS, a CCO for more than twenty-five years, remembers interviewing for a role she ultimately did not accept because the organization was a great fit, "but my potential boss was not." The boss was a senior executive, the head of finance, and he didn't have knowledge of Compliance or an apparent interest in learning more. "He had not managed Compliance before. My sense was I wouldn't have his backing." Active in industry groups, she had other opportunities she chose to pursue.

BETH SHANKER, CCO at Roubaix Capital, cautions, "Don't just think about regulatory history and the job description. At the right time, ask to meet the business leaders and the lawyers." She says applicants will get a real sense of the organization's culture by talking to more people than just those selected by the hiring manager.

JAYNTHI GANDHI, a compliance officer with more than twenty years of experience in senior roles, including as CCO, agrees with Shanker, and encourages others to ask questions about the health of the business including new product pipelines, product shelf life, and clarity of business and strategy. Compliance officers should consider business health because it can impact their ability to know whether they are a good fit for the organization. Culture is one indication of health. Compliance officers should investigate the business culture and understand attributes such as work ethic, business model agility, and pace of business developments. If a compliance officer is new to the field and looking for a less-complex environment, it may not be a good fit to join an organization with many new products that have a short two-or three-year shelf life or an organization that is transitioning and changing its strategic focus.

ANOTHER CCO at an investment company remembers a red flag from a prior job interview: four compliance officers had served in the same job over the past four years. He advises being alert for warning signs. You could either be the compliance officer that ends the excessive turnover, or become compliance officer number five out the door if you are not aligned.

CHAPTER 2 TAKEAWAY

Here's a four-step process for compliance officers to do their diligence, whether they are considering a new job or are already in a role and assessing their need to be a change agent:

1. **Get informal intel**. The organization's current and former employees and service providers are among those who can provide information.

2. **Be bold about grading the culture.** Interview the organization. Do research online but also talk with mentors and peers. Get a sense of the health and reputation of an organization. Grade its culture.

3. **Research regulatory history.** Find the results of the last independent audit or exam and how long ago it happened. Inquire about the biggest risks facing the organization. Check public websites for regulatory disclosures.

4. **Design your reporting line.** Don't just accept whatever reporting line is offered. Respectfully propose an employment arrangement to minimize conflicts and maximize your support within the business. Report to a board or independent body when possible. Confirm that you are covered by directors and officers (D&O) insurance. As a senior compliance officer, negotiate your exit in advance—if you can—with a contract and severance package: Get a contract or at least a detailed offer letter covering severance, attorney fees, etc., should you be terminated, laid off, or named in a regulatory investigation.

The resources section at the end of the book has a checklist to help with due diligence.

We have covered our first strategy for achieving Sustainable Governance: doing the research to determine whether the organization has the right alignment or to what extent it must be changed. Are employees engaged in helping Compliance, or can they be further incentivized to do so using behavioral economics? Our second strategy, covered in the next chapter, involves surveillance and technology in a trust-but-verify culture.

CHAPTER 3

VERIFYING:

I SPY AND YOU COMPLY

Kate Abbey, a veteran compliance officer for a large investment firm, starts the day, as always, with a large coffee from a local cafe. As she steps onto the trading floor, coffee in hand, her eyes wander across a sea of traders looking at their computer screens. She zeroes in on a troubling sight. The CEO is sitting at the head trader's desk. It appears the trader is looking on as the CEO is trading. Kate views this scene as a red flag, especially because the head trader looks at her anxiously. The CEO takes his eyes off his screen briefly and appears to glare at Kate as she passes by. Instead of disrupting whatever the two men are doing, she keeps walking across the floor and allows them to finish.

Imagine this: The firm is MF Global, and instead of letting them be, Kate immediately searches the surveillance system and uses the results to educate the CEO and trader. She debunks any rationalizations they offer and, in doing so, she ends up saving the organization from closing in bankruptcy.

In reality, MF Global lost more than $1 billion in client money and paid fines after years of investigation by the Commodity Futures Trading Commission for inappropriate trades. Thus, in 2011, this well-known financial services company went bankrupt. We call such crises that could or should have been foreseen "predictable surprises." Compliance officers can build a trust-but-verify culture and prevent predictable surprises. Here are three steps to build the culture using a Triple Bottom-Line Compliance System:

PROTECTION

1. **Use surveillance** to search for and find red flags. Regularly searching for any kind of aberrant customer transactions, trading or money movements, communications, or social media activity will turn up issues, if they exist. Compliance officers guard the organization from regulatory enforcement by using surveillance to find and fix problems before they draw attention from others.

PRODUCTIVITY

2. **Be analytical**, looking at things holistically, connecting the dots, and knowing business patterns as well as individuals' traits if that is a practical consideration in the organization. Simultaneously find issues and opportunities to improve work flow, products, and services.

IMPACT

3. **Collaborate** with others in the organization to double-check any findings to make sure they reflect a real or potential compliance breach, not false alarms, and if so, go directly to the source of the risk as an advisor and an educator. Compliance officers can build a credible brand for accuracy and thoughtful policing. They will be better prepared to make an impact on the culture, educating executives and incentivizing them to act when needed.

To take the first step, a compliance officer must have state-of-the-art technology tools. Just as spies have sophisticated tools for surveillance, rather than paper and pens, compliance officers need tools that are aligned with contemporary expectations. Those expectations are rapidly advancing to keep pace with innovations in technology. Trends in regulatory and financial services automation, known as RegTech and FinTech, are changing the way we work, improving productivity for compliance officers and others. The innovation in automation has taken hold globally, and compliance officers must advocate to make sure tools are available so they can monitor their Clients' behavior.

Government regulators, including securities industry regulators and the US Department of Justice, continue to invest in technology, adopting their own cyber initiatives in which they have been spending millions of dollars on surveillance technology to ferret out fraud and hackers. The government, to ensure that consumers are protected, will pressure regulated organizations to have equally good surveillance tools. Organizations cannot prevent fraud if they can't find it. Without surveillance technology, compliance officers are dependent on employees to self-report data, and then Compliance spends a lot of time capturing, sorting, and filing that data.

Data generated from high-tech surveillance doesn't provide a full picture by itself. To achieve Sustainable Governance—to have Compliance make an impact by preventing predictable surprises—also requires sophisticated data analytics within the surveillance tools. The government has invested in those efforts too, and companies need to catch up. Compliance officers should either have or hire the technical expertise to build those analytics.

Voice of Experience

ANDREW SIEGEL, the CCO for an investment firm focused on blockchain technology, reminds compliance officers that partnering with the Information Technology (IT) team is equally as important as partnering with business colleagues. In this scenario, it'll be paramount to build a conflicts-of-interest process—you'll need to reconcile the organization's data regarding employees and executives against client data. If you have inaccurate or delayed client data, conflicts will go unidentified, potentially harming clients or others.

Siegel offers advice to compliance officers: Before pitching the purchase of new technology, ask your IT team to help you determine whether your vendors or in-house IT department can help leverage existing capabilities with existing data. If not, as you transfer legacy data to new systems, you'll need to ensure that the integrity of the data is not compromised. If you have inaccurate or incomplete data regarding personal investments of employees or client portfolio holdings, conflicts may go unidentified. Remember: compliance officers need accurate data to review, reconcile, and investigate compliance issues to prevent actual conflicts or the appearance of impropriety. Ultimately, your surveillance is "only as good as the data being captured." Garbage in, garbage out.

To make sure you have valid, comprehensive data inputs for surveillance, plan ahead and set expectations about ownership, access, and transparency to data and any data warehouse. If IT and developers think of Compliance as a "need to know" stakeholder, your efforts will be slowed and potentially lead to ineffective surveillance with false positives or failed issue discovery. Compliance "needs to travel at the speed of business," Siegel reminds us. Rather than rely on intermediaries to understand data, you should be aware of—and avoid—any "black box" arrangements. Instead, have early discussions about data integrity.

Handling data inventories, assessments, and access is an important governance issue. Compliance officers need to know who owns, has a stake in, and can query the data and data warehouse, in addition to where the data and data warehouse come from.

Compliance officers need a seat at the table to help design effective data management programs so there is an uncomplicated way to use, sort, and query the data, including any databases. How easy? Think of the ease of using Google as a standard. If you hit resistance in the data management process, realign and persevere by adopting your resistor's perspective. Don't fight City Hall. Go with the business flow and incentives. Partner and get full transparency to data.

Smart surveillance tools rely on the principles of behavioral economics. To incentivize good business judgment, ethical behavior, and engagement with the Compliance program, employees need to understand that their behavior will be monitored. In a trust-but-verify company culture, Compliance manages and addresses the drivers of employees' rationalized behavior. Most commonly in an organization, anyone who diverges from business ethics is relying on self-deception and one or both of two rationalizations: "Everyone else is doing it," and, "I'm not harming anyone." (For supporting research by behavioral economist Dan Ariely, see the resources section.) An effective surveillance program not only has to regularly find those rationalized behaviors, but also give feedback to the employees, showing them the harm and making them see that everyone else is *not* doing it. By sharing results of a broad surveillance program, Compliance educates the workforce about both risks and rationalizations.

Smart surveillance tools, all while running behind the scenes, provide critical self-analysis for an organization, don't burden employees with data collection and disclosure work, and find problems early enough so they can be fixed.

Critical self-analysis means you find your problems before someone else does. For a compliance officer, finding an issue before a customer, regulator, or the public becomes aware of it is the key to providing not only protection but also value for the organization. Moving from bare compliance, or bureaucratic information collection, to a system that runs smoothly behind the scenes and finds problems early has obvious value. But getting the resources to successfully make that transition is a common challenge for Compliance in competition with infrastructure needs on the client-facing side. Sometimes compliance officers are so focused on covering risk and protection they're not able to look at the longer-term impact they could have by keeping up with evolving technology. And if they don't keep pace, the risk of ineffective surveillance becomes more serious. So the rest of this chapter will discuss in depth making a case for more resources.

As of the time this book is being written, many Compliance programs have some catching up to do compared with the technology available to regulators. It's a dangerous situation if regulators highlight information the company executives don't know about their own business or employees' conduct. When you think about our personal lives and how easily we can get information on our mobile devices and web searches, it's reasonable to expect that getting Compliance information also should be handy, simple, and elegant. The compliance officers who have not put a business case together to earn their place in the hierarchy of their organization's technical spending priorities, or who are passively waiting for the regulators to tell them what they need because they rationalize they don't have the support of the business need to update their approach have an outdated method of thinking. This chapter covers strategies for how to change your approach and catch up.

Voice of Experience

VAUGHN SWARTZ, a seasoned executive of North America Compliance at Rabobank, reminds us, "It takes more time and commitment" to influence the business without the crutch of regulatory risk scare tactics. It may be a comfortable shortcut to think Compliance requests must be accepted outright because they relate to legal requirements. However, compliance officers are better served when they use the same framework the business uses to justify an investment in IT or a new initiative. This is an opportunity for compliance officers to demonstrate business acumen and alignment with business needs. Before pitching for resources or a policy change, compliance officers should do the research and put a business case together illustrating the impact to—and perhaps operational improvements for—the business.

Swartz encourages compliance officers who feel they don't have adequate support and influence to consider whether their message is getting lost in translation. Busy compliance officers may prioritize firefighting over communicating within the organization or rely too heavily on regulatory scare tactics. As a result, they suffer with a tainted reputation that they are too conservative and don't understand how to accept and mitigate business risks. Compliance officers should communicate not just more frequently, but more strategically. They can incentivize buy-in by focusing on how Compliance can add value—creating efficiencies, finding process improvements, and building a productive governance framework.

Getting an organization to spend money on surveillance technology comes down to three steps: (1) the need, (2) the ask, and (3) the plan.

A compliance officer should be prepared to make a compelling business case about why the organization needs to spend money on surveillance technology. That technology will be the heart of the entire Compliance program, and it's typically expensive.

The "ask" should be presented as a fulsome, positive business case, not just as a proclamation that the organization must spend the money to comply with the law. A compliance officer must be able to explain from a business perspective what problems the technology is going to solve. We all know it's possible to minimally comply with the law using outdated technology or handling information manually. Asking to be placed higher up in the hierarchy of budget dollars requires a specific forecast of value for the money spent.

It's also crucial to develop an implementation plan because incorrectly integrated technology may increase risks and bureaucracy and waste money. Without a plan, implementation can be ineffective either because it produces too many false positives, or because it is not actually looking for what everyone thinks it should be looking for. A compliance officer who is solely an advisor—perhaps a cerebral, analytical personality—is not going to be easily trusted to handle millions of dollars of software spending. A compliance officer must show he or she is not only a smart advisor, but also a pragmatic and capable project manager who knows how to implement and calibrate a new system or get the help to do so.

Making sure the money is well spent is also in the best interest of the compliance officer. Often in the past, compliance officers have won a budget for new software, either because the regulators required it or because they successfully made a pitch and they didn't understand the technology or were too busy firefighting to ensure proper implementation. So then the surveillance didn't work, they missed the red flags, and they failed to prevent a crisis like the one described at the beginning of this chapter.

Once established, surveillance technology requires continuing attention, maintenance, and support to keep it functioning as needed. At least annually, if not quarterly, someone should check to make sure each system is optimized. If the data that's coming in and out—the actual engine of the surveillance—is not operating as expected or circumstances have changed, it must be recalibrated.

Voice of Experience

Early in my career, I learned a lesson from a mentor when I was frustrated, lacking confidence, and worrying on a particularly busy day about some open risks. **GEORGE SCHIEREN,** a prominent figure in the New York financial and legal communities, simply asked, "Beth, do you have a plan?"

Schieren had been the general counsel and senior vice president of Merrill Lynch when it was the biggest brokerage in the United States. Before that, he served as the chief of branch enforcement, and then the assistant regional administrator of the New York Regional Office of the Securities and Exchange Commission. His advice was that almost any issue is manageable once you create a plan and begin to implement it.

When you set out all the issues in a project plan, you not only prioritize your own work, but the plan helps you communicate and get the momentum from others in the organization that you need.

A plan makes it easier to gain early buy-in from all the different stakeholders as the compliance officer gets them engaged by seeking information and then uses the information to keep the plan aligned with the business. As any businessperson would do for a new product launch, the compliance officer must prioritize budget and time for each program component and show ROI. There are always a multitude of daily issues and time pressures to deal with in Compliance, but having a plan helps a compliance officer manage his or her career by showing progress in a major project. Compliance programs aren't designed to be static; they should always evolve and move forward.

An image that sums up a theme of this book is the "Circle of Compliance." The circle is an example of a compliance officer's ability to not just protect, but also to add value with a Triple Bottom-Line Compliance System that continuously addresses employees' and management's behavioral rationalizations. Smart surveillance yields valuable information, so a compliance officer can show the business the direct harm of violations and what's working and what isn't, which in turn improves other parts of the Compliance program. When the compliance officer finds out what's working well and what isn't, he or she learns where training, outreach, and communication about policy are required. The compliance officer may find an issue and use it to figure out what is changing in the business or regulatory environment. It's a virtuous cycle, and surveillance is the fuel that keeps it in motion. Compliance officers can leverage the results of testing, auditing, and electronic surveillance to build a governance framework that is customized to the organization and sustainable regardless of inevitable changes to the business, client needs, and industry trends.

In pitching for surveillance resources or explaining the complexities of good governance, this fluid image is a fantastic visual to show stakeholders the Compliance program is always a work in progress. Regardless of whether the program covers five people or five thousand, it should include monitoring and surveillance, one of the best ways to find a compliance gap before it turns into a systemic problem.

CIRCLE OF COMPLIANCE

Each step in the Circle of Compliance should involve making a persuasive pitch for technology resources. A strong business case makes saying "yes" to the request easy because it defines the *need* in relation to the business and industry expectations while forecasting *results* with and without technology.

Benchmarking will be a vital component of a pitch. To build a reputation as a compliance officer who can be trusted to spend responsibly, use common sense and good business judgment when pitching. Even if the organization has embarked on a massive new initiative, the need for the new technology is obvious, or resources aren't tight, the compliance officer still should build a solid business case.

The chart on the next page shows the various steps in the Circle of Compliance, and the results that can be expected without or with a Triple Bottom-Line technology solution. Although technology for each step contributes to a more effective Compliance cycle overall, every request may not be approved, so top priorities should be pitched first.

CIRCLE OF COMPLIANCE STEP	MANUAL OPTION WITHOUT TECHNOLOGY	MANUAL OPTION RESULTS
Analysis of requirements	Check regulator websites	• Reactive, may not be consistently tracked, may be behind the industry
Policy outreach and communication	E-mail blasts	• May get lost in e-mail boxes and may not be read or won't be available on demand when employee is looking for an answer • Need to dedicate resources to audits of compliance record keeping
Training and on-demand advisory	E-mail certifications, online external courses	• Cost savings: may trade engagement and effectiveness and perception of bureaucracy with off-the-shelf content
Monitoring and surveillance	Random sampling, excel spreadsheet exception reports	• Siloed view for monitoring, management reporting, and information may be more like data collection than analysis • Need to conduct audits to confirm adequacy of manual processes
Changes to business and regulatory environment	E-mail, news, networking	• Respond as needed: ad hoc surgical responses • Need to conduct audits to confirm adequacy of manual processes

TRIPLE BOTTOM-LINE TECHNOLOGY SOLUTION	TECHNOLOGY SOLUTION RESULTS
• Automatic alerts from sources • Maintain central electronic inventory or data warehouse of advice (not personal files)	• Save money and time not reassessing same question or missing a trend • Leverage prior work and efficiencies • Meet industry and regulatory expectations
• Information portal • Online resource library and outreach • Record keeping is automated	• Increase effectiveness of communications • On-demand resources available • Increase engagement and decrease confusion on standards • Meet industry and regulatory expectations and build a competitive advantage
• Compliance dashboard • One-stop outreach on portal • Videos and tailored training content debunking any rationalizations that get in the way of responsible corporate behavior	• Increase effectiveness of communications • Increase engagement and decrease confusion on standards • Meet industry and regulatory expectations and build a competitive advantage
• Integrated IT • Artificial intelligence • Data hub/warehouse for employee matters and business exception monitoring	• Systemic assessments to enable strategic risk assessments • Stay ahead of regulators and brand compliance officer reputation • Meet industry and regulatory expectations and build a competitive advantage
• Risk matrices, assessments, and testing • Value matrices and management reporting	• Manage and measure regulatory risks in the same manner as financial risks • Meet industry and regulatory expectations • Build a competitive advantage by tracking value-add in the same manner as regulatory risk

Voices of Experience

LISA CROSSLEY, the executive director of the National Society for Compliance Professionals (NSCP), advises a compliance officer master not just a surveillance program, but also the entire Circle of Compliance. A compliance officer who "keeps adjusting" and "doesn't get too comfortable" will be closer to designing a surveillance program that delivers a seamless result, simple and productive like a Google search. To reach that point, the compliance officer must always be thinking, "Let's see what we can do better." The compliance officer does not need to be an IT expert, but educated and confident enough in technology to hire an expert for the team.

Crossley reminds compliance officers to leverage others to advocate for needed resources. The plan will succeed more easily if senior management or a sympathetic colleague in another department can help the compliance officer or even pitch the need for resources for Compliance.

DENNIS KELLEHER, the CCO of the Align Impact investing firm, encourages compliance officers to prepare to "sell the sizzle." He advises starting with, "Here's what the technology saves us," showing productivity and impact before the protection leg of Triple Bottom-Line Compliance. Then cover an enforcement case for a company that was penalized for similar failures at surveillance. Show what it costs an organization in reputational capital and money and time defending regulatory matters. In his approach, compliance officers focus on their business acumen, selling

and marketing in a very visual way to have people understand their priorities and empathize with Compliance.

Previously, the beginning, middle, and end of the technology
sales pitch for some compliance officers was, "Regulators expect it,
so we need it." Compliance officers who "sell the sizzle," in Kelleher's words, have a better story to tell. For example, if compliance
officers want money for an upgraded code of conduct system, they
will explain that for the same money the organization also will be
able to identify policy breaches and Finance and Human Resources
problems because the system will ferret out misappropriation of
funds, disengaged and unproductive employees, and policy violations. The system will make the overall organization more efficient
and, by the way, meet the expectations of regulators. **In industries
less regulated than financial services, a code of ethics and conduct
is equally important.** The Circle of Compliance prevents conflicts
of interest, insider trading, and violations of labor and employment
laws. Global manufacturing companies implement "trust-but-verify"
strategies to also comply with anti-bribery laws and responsible
supply chain standards.

Compliance professionals should clearly define surveillance
objectives, the issues they want to monitor, and red flags for escala-
tion. They must design a system framework even if they are not IT
experts. Without planning, when compliance officers launch into IT
discussions, it may seem like Compliance professionals are speaking
Swahili and IT colleagues are speaking Russian. They should work
to find a common language and understanding of the technology
objectives. Compliance officers who master better collaboration will
also master implementation.

When technology resources are committed, and implementation planning is underway, a compliance officer's strategic involvement is still necessary. This is closer to the beginning than the end of a compliance officer's work. Technology that isn't properly tailored and integrated can be just as ineffective and inefficient as relying on manual processes and chance to find issues.

In Compliance, a balky system or one that results in excessive false results builds unnecessary bureaucracy and stymies productivity. A team that builds a bare compliance surveillance system may return with a plan that involves reconciling different spreadsheets kept by different people, and then emailing the results. That kind of system appears to guard against regulatory enforcement risks, but there's too much room for error. The team should be sent back to create or find a single, analytical system that is tailored to collect, analyze, and display defined information. It should provide alerts, maybe literal red flags.

Surveillance implementation is an art worth mastering. Without it, a compliance officer won't have meaningful testing, audits, and surveillance results to leverage. A trust-but-verify culture depends on Compliance receiving those tailored results. If a software system that helps monitor e-mails, texts, and chat boxes has not turned up anything to investigate after a month, the surveillance technology probably requires calibration. Those in charge of implementation should adjust it to include random and risk-based sample groups and further customize the screening logic in the system.

There might be pressure to build a system to meet regulatory requirements in a short amount of time, but if it's done without planning and the early help of IT, the involvement of business managers, and counsel, money could be wasted. As in any system implementation in business, it pays to have a cross-functional team, a pilot project before launch, and a well-thought-out plan. Some common pitfalls that result from lack of proper planning are unbudgeted additional costs, delays because of resistance, and inelegant solutions that don't address the risks because of a lack of operational understanding.

To avoid those pitfalls, compliance officers should enlist a team of business managers, employees, Legal, and IT, and seek comment and buy-in, early and often. Those collaborators will help select customized surveillance rules that match business priorities, such as a new marketing campaign or problem areas with underperforming sales teams, in addition to generic industry concerns about fraud or promised guarantees. Collaboration not only gives Compliance a way to leverage surveillance more widely within the organization's ecosystem, but it also produces information for use in targeting training, controls, and employee incentives.

Avoid implementation pitfalls with extraordinary focus on project organization and planning. Make a plan and stick to it. Avoid getting overwhelmed and missing important conduct, culture, and governance risks because of delays or mistakes. Plan and prioritize implementation by assessing the exposure or risk if surveillance isn't effective.

Finally, the surveillance plan should include management reporting on implementation to stakeholders showing the ROI. This reporting on the value of the technology will enhance the compliance officer's reputation as a responsible leader building a productive governance culture. When it's time to start the cycle again, to upgrade or enhance the system, Compliance has a track record of operating like a business and showing a ROI on surveillance technology.

HOW WOULD YOU RISK-RATE THE SURVEILLANCE PROJECTS IN THE CHART BELOW FOR YOUR OWN ORGANIZATION?

The first column shows what needs to be verified. The second column shows what is under surveillance, and the third column shows how the surveillance works for each item. As a conversation starter, the team implementing surveillance can rate each verification item high, medium, or low priority.

VERIFY	BASIC CONTROLS	SURVEILLANCE TECHNOLOGY
Employee conduct	• Written policies • Disclosures • Training • Certifications	Analyze, reconcile, and monitor for red flags: • Electronic communications and social media • Outside business interests • Political contributions • Cash and non-cash incentives and gifts • Code of ethics and conduct
Business conflicts	• Written policies • Disclosures • Training • Certifications	Analyze, reconcile, and monitor for red flags: • Design and delivery of services/products • Performance and financial incentives • Profits ahead of duties such as trading, providing advice, and supply chain standards
Fraud and financial crimes	• Written policies • Disclosures • Training • Certifications	Analyze, reconcile, and monitor for red flags: • Financial controls for misappropriation • Electronic communications and social media • Anti-money laundering (AML) • Anti-bribery

CHAPTER 3 TAKEAWAY

We've now covered the strategy of testing in a trust-but-verify system. A well-planned surveillance program promotes Sustainable Governance because it not only covers legal requirements, but also helps with productivity. It produces valuable information and can help a company avoid the predictable surprises that result in crises or scandals. To ask for resources for such a system, a compliance officer must engage stakeholders, get their buy-in, learn about the business needs, and plan for project implementation. Collaboration must continue through the implementation process so the system can be adjusted to meet business needs and produce value. The next chapter goes deeper into the dynamics of collaboration between Compliance and the rest of the organization as we look at the strategy for serving clients.

CHAPTER 4

MANAGING YOUR HYDRA

E very lush leather chair at the power table is occupied. The compliance officer is describing to twenty-five manicured, middle-aged men that their elite education isn't enough. For Compliance reasons, they need more training and credentialing. The most senior, supposedly well-mannered man impulsively blurts out, "You're crazy."

That kind of skepticism about Compliance is often unspoken but needs to be understood and managed by compliance officers. We are all aware that our work can—and in many cases is designed to—break the rhythm of business. That's why adding business value with Compliance work is so crucial to achieve sustainable, respected results.

Compliance officers are not always able to focus on risks specific to their organization. Sometimes, compliance officers must lead mandates prescribed by laws, rules, and regulations that haven't kept pace with technology or the business environment. Relationships—the focus of this chapter—are especially important in these scenarios.

Compliance work, with its varied and sometimes conflicting duties, can seem so Herculean at times that it calls to mind the Greek myth of the Hydra, a monster with many heads. Cut off one head and two more emerge. A compliance officer must have thick skin, composure, and an ability to read people and deal with big egos to manage the Hydra. Many compliance officers are analytical by nature, which is important, but relationships and communication skills are what make a good compliance officer great. A compliance officer who can develop and master a project plan so that the work is high quality and completed on time will earn influence. Extraordinary compliance officers are business leaders, strategists, and project managers; they are influencers that can get things done.

For example, compliance officers can add value as they manage surveillance system implementation, as we discussed in chapter 3, or when they find a compliance issue, address underlying systemic weaknesses, and take opportunities to make improvements and educate. This approach is the opposite of "don't make waves," and "not my job," attitudes.

Voice of Experience

A CHIEF COMPLIANCE OFFICER for a large mutual fund complex discovers an error. He explains here how, in addition of remediating the error, he investigates ways to guard against repeated errors and find opportunities to increase productivity and employee engagement.

This investigation involves four steps:

1. Finding out how the error happened

2. Researching whether written protocols existed, and if so, whether they were followed

3. Investigating whether there were obvious alerts or a pattern of less-obvious alerts, and how employees reacted to those alerts, and

4. Studying why the incident happened and whether improving some processes could prevent a repeat of that same error.

The investigation goes further than just asking how and why the error happened, because the compliance officer is showing leadership and adding value to Compliance.

It can be particularly difficult for compliance officers to effectively show how they add value when they must enforce a regulation that seems outdated or irrelevant to their business. Unfortunately, that burden sometimes comes with the gatekeeper role that compliance officers play on behalf of regulators. Communicating Compliance needs often means delivering costly or negative news and dealing with strong reactions. Just like a psychoanalyst, compliance officers should understand the personalities they're dealing with, listening— and almost mirroring their language and preferences—to build a relationship. Strong leaders in an organization often have big egos, so the compliance officer may feel like a psychoanalyst with a clientele of celebrities. The compliance officer must put his or her ego aside and have the empathy to understand what drives and incentivizes the leader's behavior.

A compliance officer is well served by acknowledging and actively managing potentially conflicting loyalties as a gatekeeper and a business leader within an organization. On one hand, a compliance officer is expected to be client-centric within the organization, but on the other hand he has an obligation to also manage those clients as a gatekeeper for regulators. Compliance officers have responsibilities to bosses, peers, and legal departments. So, in some sense, the simple term "client" doesn't reflect this context and is misleading. **I coined the term "Glient" to reflect the complexity of compliance officers' relationships within an organization.** Internal stakeholders come to them and ask for advice and guidance as clients, but the compliance officers are equally responsible for reporting to the regulators and serving as regulatory gatekeepers. Regulators can sanction compliance officers in ways that range from criticism to criminal prosecution.

To manage your Hydra, it may help to jettison the term "clients" and think in terms of "Glients."

The gatekeeper role can make its presence known in unexpected and dramatic ways. For example, a compliance officer in Chicago for a national firm gets what appears to be a routine phone message to call someone named Bonnie Farmer in Jacksonville. When Bonnie picks up, she says, "Let me put you on speakerphone." Suddenly, the compliance officer is speaking on a recorded call with five officials, including heads of the Florida enforcement division. They speak in a polite but aggressive tone—"Do you agree to be recorded? We need to treat this call as evidence." In this case, the firm has made statements about products on its new website that adhere to federal regulations, but state officials want to take a tougher stance. And they treat the compliance officer as though he is the one who created the website and is making commissions off product sales in Florida. A compliance officer is well served in such a situation by knowing as much as possible about the business, its products, and its people.

GLIENT HYDRA

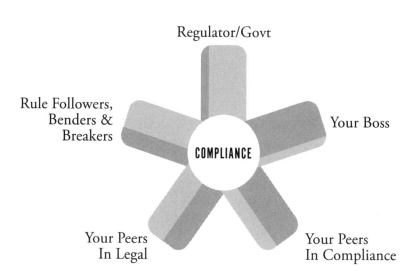

CLIENT   GATEKEEPER

Regulator/Govt

Rule Followers,
Benders &
Breakers

Your Boss

COMPLIANCE

Your Peers
In Legal

Your Peers
In Compliance

Voice of Experience

Earlier in my career, a brilliant businesswoman with extraordinary people skills taught me to know my client and adjust accordingly. **KATHRYN GEORGE,** a partner at Brown Brothers Harriman & Co., taught me an important starting point for understanding clients is to expect differing views of Compliance and its ability to incentivize good business judgment. With a smile and a curious mind, she helped the Compliance team build rapport and reminded us that a compliance officer who doesn't understand varying behaviors and simply announces edicts will have a tough time making a sustainable impact on anyone's business judgment.

Compliance officers must manage three major types of occasionally hard-to-please Clients. Years ago, a mentor encouraged me to build rapport with business leaders by understanding their inclinations to think like a **Rule Follower**, **Rule Bender**, or **Rule Breaker**. This is an intentionally exaggerated or oversimplified typology for private use only, but it helps remind a compliance officer to master multiple points of view that may change with each new topic and businessperson. The compliance officer must adapt a communication style to fit the audience in one-on-ones, small groups, or complex multi-stakeholder projects. What follows is advice addressed directly to compliance officers on how to use the typology as an informal way to empathize with the Clients' perspective.

GLIENT PROCLIVITY	GLIENT PERSPECTIVE ON COMPLIANCE OFFICERS	STRATEGIES FOR COMPLIANCE OFFICERS
Rule Followers	Trusted advisor	Keep pace with regulatory developments and anticipate evolving regulatory risks.
Rule Benders	Trusted gun	Same as Rule Followers but be aware of True North Ethics, and advise on good business judgment and ethics. See chapter 8.
Rule Breakers	Not easily trusted	Same as Rule Followers and Benders but also consult with outside advisors as needed.

Some businesspeople are **Rule Followers**. As a compliance officer, you are easily a trusted advisor to Rule Followers. The Rule Followers will seek your advice. It's important to maintain these relationships by keeping current with regulatory developments and best practices. Serve as their proactive advisor. Anticipate a Rule Follower's needs with third-eye skills that help you build the foundation for your Sustainable Governance model. This strategy will allow you to bring sustainable value to the organization while reducing conduct risk, a risk that quick fixes or technical, bare compliance can never fully address. If you reduce conduct risk, you can make a lasting impact on an organization and be part of a Triple Bottom-Line Compliance program that avoids systemic Compliance issues and helps deliver organizational growth and stability.

Rule Benders tend to cherish innovation. These leaders come to compliance officers for clever support. When advising Rule Benders, you should document facts supporting your advice. Clearly highlight risks, especially when best practices and rules are not well-defined. It's important to serve as a business ethics ombudsman when providing advice to Rule Benders. It's crucial to give Rule Benders two responses—one that addresses the requirements and one that explains any uncertain territory and business ethics considerations. Your ethics may be tested as Rule Benders look for an angle you missed, so prepare and consider any ethical questions before providing your advice.

Voice of Experience

MARY TOUMPAS worked as the CCO at a newly launched organization that was proud of its innovative start-up culture. It was led by inexperienced Rule Benders who also lacked market perspective. As the organization hadn't yet experienced down markets, its risk structure was unproven. Toumpas, as one of its first CCOs, faced this challenge by "constantly trying to educate the business about the rules." She was able to make an impact with those who "were thirsty for knowledge and were open to education." She did the research, prepared, and then "painted the box" from within which the Rule Benders could operate. Of course, they constantly came back to see if the shape could be changed, but the Sustainable Governance culture grew and evolved because the business learned, and they felt comfortable understanding the boundaries she had helped set.

It's always important to collaborate, build a consensus, and escalate issues to your manager. To protect your credibility, it is even more important to do so before providing advice to Rule Benders who, if they aren't wildly excited about your answer, may seek out a second opinion potentially from your manager.

Rarely will you encounter **Rule Breakers**. But when you do, be confident, prepared, and equally strategic and exactingly tactical. Advising Rule Breakers often entails carefully preparing and confidently negotiating even the most routine matters. Often, conversations reflect either the Rule Breaker's doubts that the compliance requirement brings value to the organization, or they have a blind spot about their own conduct.

Before engaging in a debate with a Rule Breaker, prepare by putting a precise pin through the facts. Know your business, the law or regulation, and the distinction between the best practice and the technical requirement. Enable Rule Breakers to defer to you in private. Whenever possible, initially address topics outside formal meetings to avoid unproductive power struggles. Leave your ego aside and meet Rule Breakers in their comfort zone. **Try to build a personal relationship or rapport that can be strategically leveraged to facilitate discussions.** You may need outside help to check your boundaries and personal risks in this undoubtedly tough environment. Remember to lean on your external and internal network to check on whether you are delivering on your gatekeeper role.

A Rule Breaker is not likely to reflexively trust a compliance officer as a valued advisor. The compliance officer's ego will be tested because the role ultimately may not be respected. To be effective, you will need to accept that you may not have visible authority within an organization. That means day-to-day you will not easily be included in strategic business initiatives. Instead, you may be brought in late in the development process, so you may be at a disadvantage initially when it comes to researching and providing commercially viable and ethical solutions. It will be important to invite yourself to meetings, rely on getting information informally from peers and your boss, and reiterate early and often the need for communication to get better results from you as an advisor. If you leave your ego at the door, you can still get the job done. This is not a one-person job, though. Get help from a good Friends of Compliance (FOC) network, as explained further in the next chapter. Vet your advice through your peers, boss, and outside experts whenever possible, and fully bake any advice with smart operational solutions and surveillance.

Voice of Experience

LARRY BLOCK, the CCO for C-III Investment Management, reminds compliance officers to adjust their approach when supporting business leaders who prioritize "optionality" and discretion. Business leaders may have substantial experience and even legal training. So, when they advise these leaders, compliance officers must understand that they need to give more than rule-based answers. Compliance officers must provide industry context, the rationale for the requirement, and consider a flexible Compliance process designed to enable business discretion. Such a process often requires more documentation and additional case-by-case approvals.

Block recalls a time early in his career when his business leaders were senior and experienced. They expected to be able to use good business judgment as they launched a new, non-US product. In researching the Compliance issues, he knew almost immediately that he had to address the challenge that non-US requirements were inflexible rules without room for business judgment. The business leaders needed to accept the confined structure if they wanted to launch the product. Fortunately, they brought him into the process early, so there were no surprises. Early engagement makes collaboration with any type of Glient easier.

There's a natural conflict between Compliance and Rule Breakers that can emerge in surprising ways, even at a social gathering. The Rule Breakers have a stereotyped view of the compliance officer as someone they shouldn't trust or get close to. When the compliance officer tries to build rapport, the Rule Breaker acts out to put up a barrier. So, the compliance officer shows up at a company cocktail party, and the Rule Breakers start talking about how much fun it would be to take him outside and throw him into the swimming pool.

In the absence of good relationships, a compliance officer will have less influence and more difficulty getting the job done. Suppose a compliance officer makes an urgent call from Boston to the London office for some information needed to respond to a request by regulators. The internal client in London seems to be in a hurry to get off the phone, raising suspicions of wrongdoing. There is a tense back-and-forth. Eventually, the compliance officer realizes that it's Valentine's Day and five hours ahead in London, and the client just wants to get out of the office for a date, but they didn't have the rapport for such an honest explanation of personal priorities.

CHAPTER 4 TAKEAWAY

This chapter covered the strategy of serving a Glient. We have seen that compliance officers need to understand and manage skepticism about their dual role as a gatekeeper for regulators and a client-centric advisor. Developing project management skills and relating to different personalities will help compliance officers be influential. Understanding distinct types of Glients—those who follow, bend, or break rules—enables a compliance officer to show empathy and adapt communication to different audiences. A compliance officer doesn't have to go it alone in dealing with hard-to-please Glients, however, if the compliance officer follows the networking strategy explained in the next chapter.

CHAPTER 5

NETWORKING: FRIENDS DON'T LET FRIENDS GET BLAMED

ate one evening, Roger Pike is in his office when he receives a courtesy call from the regulators that enforcement charges are coming. The routine exam he was managing as a compliance officer is now serious and personal. The charges will involve significant regulatory rule violations against the organization. Pike is stunned to find out he is also personally named in the case. The regulator has determined the company's Compliance program failed. Pike is sitting there wondering, "How did I get here? I didn't steal or lie. I tried my best when I hit matters of interpretation. I thought we were covered." Pike recalls the heated debate with colleagues: the lawyers, the legal memos, and the compromising. There were healthy discussions about who should be accountable for follow-up. Despite all the energy expended, somehow the regulators believe, with the benefit of hindsight, the compliance officer compromised too much. They view the charges as a way of sending a message to other compliance officers that Pike was negligent in carrying out the gatekeeper duties.

A crisis like what Pike, the fictional compliance officer, faced doesn't happen in a day. It results not from one misjudgment but a prolonged period of give-and-take within a company and focusing on clients instead of Glients. The day-by-day workflow of questions, issues, projects, and resolutions can lead to conflicts of interest and a crisis. To prevent such a risk, the compliance officer must constantly manage his or her professional brand, reputation, and a Triple Bottom-Line Compliance System. For example, and as we will cover in this chapter, being diligent and finding and fixing errors saves a compliance officer and the organization the embarrassment of providing sloppy, inaccurate affirmations which can be a red flag for regulators looking for personal accountability when something does go wrong.

Voice of Experience

JANINE DILJOHN, CCO at an alternative investment manager, notes that each compliance officer brings his or her own approach to the role. But, she says, "You can't have an effective Compliance program if people don't talk to you and you don't know the business." A compliance officer must manage their reputation by understanding the spirit of the business and building a reputation for supporting the business while simultaneously serving as a gatekeeper. For example, when it comes to approving marketing campaigns, Diljohn encourages compliance officers to collaborate and ask what the business is trying to accomplish before immediately editing the marketing material or prohibiting its use.

A compliance officer who can look at issues and materials through the eyes of colleagues is most likely to add value. A compliance officer with a reputation for being pragmatic and innovative has conversations instead of debates with others in the organization. The conversations lead to results that protect the integrity and reputation of the compliance officer, the organization, and the business.

Compliance officers must keep up with regulatory expectations and norms, but they are more than governance experts. They're also business leaders, employees, and thought leaders. To protect their brand and add value to their organization, compliance officers should build and manage an internal and an external community. A compliance officer needs to understand industry trends and use that intelligence to develop smart ways to address challenges. In other words, successful compliance officers manage their reputation 360 degrees:

- In their industry, they participate in groups and keep abreast of developments.

- With Compliance, Legal, and risk peers, they seek help and collaboration.

- With business leaders, they build a network of "Friends of Compliance" (FOCs) to help point out red flags and provide candid feedback about their ideas and work.

- With the boss and board, they gain protectors before risk of blaming sets in.

Regulators and others have held compliance officers personally accountable for what is labeled, with the benefit of hindsight, as negligence. Neither regulators nor plaintiffs' counsel will be persuaded by the defense that the compliance officer didn't have enough resources, support, or time. For instance, before signing regulatory filings, client certifications, auditor requests, and management representation letters, compliance officers must perform due diligence. Regardless of deadlines, they must require backup, documentation, or supporting certifications if culturally acceptable. If the information provided under the compliance officer's signature is later determined to be inaccurate, the documentation shows the compliance officer was not negligent. When developing policies, the compliance officer should adopt a Triple Bottom-Line approach and confirm they adequately cover risks from an operational—as well as business and regulatory—perspective.

Voice of Experience

JAYNTHI GANDHI, the CCO introduced in chapter 2, advises: "Always understand what you are signing. Know why you are signing a document and what it means." Anyone asking for an affirmation expects that all claims, data, and statistics will be substantiated. If the substantiation doesn't happen before it hits the compliance officer's desk, then the compliance officer should "ask questions and interview all the stakeholders," even if it means a deadline is missed. The firm and its clients expect the highest quality of review and diligence. Check data, make sure it is mined from the correct data warehouse, and make sure you understand the operational workflows and risks before you sign. More often than not, compliance officer due diligence leads to finding and fixing errors.

So how does a compliance officer get the resources, support, and time for due diligence? A network of "Friends of Compliance" (FOCs) within a company can provide diverse perspectives, identify issues, and help a compliance officer build smart controls. A solo compliance officer will have a tough time making an organizational impact. But research shows there is a common behavioral pattern, called a social exchange, that compliance officers can leverage to help build their FOC network. Social exchange theory essentially states that through a series of interactions, employees build a state of reciprocal interdependence, which leads to mutually beneficial trust relationships.

"Relationships evolve over time into trusting, loyal, mutual commitments, as long as the parties abide by certain rules of exchange."

— ALAN M. SAKS, "ANTECEDENTS AND CONSEQUENCES OF EMPLOYEE ENGAGEMENT."[3]

A compliance officer builds an FOC network to increase engagement in the Compliance program. Increased employee engagement in organizations has been shown to help achieve Sustainable Governance. The FOCs highlight blind spots, operational challenges, and obstacles that lead to ineffective policies and controls. A compliance officer must be a diplomat, understanding many different stakeholders. A network of FOCs can facilitate development of that understanding by being a source of information about business perspectives, strategy, and priorities. The support network thereby becomes a compliance officer's secret weapon, boosting diplomacy skills before important presentations or requests for resources. Time spent building an FOC network helps the organization and the compliance officer's reputation.

---

3   Alan M. Saks, "Antecedents and Consequences of Employee Engagement," *Journal of Managerial Psychology* 21, no. 7 (2006): 600-619.

A compliance officer's people skills, willingness to give back value and be supportive of the business, and ability to network are important components of a Sustainable Governance system in which employees self-report to Compliance. But from a systemic perspective, Compliance must also work with management and Human Resources to incentivize that cooperation. Employees' contributions to Sustainable Governance should be considered during annual performance appraisals and compensation decisions. Did they complete their training? Did they find process improvements or predictable surprises? Did they help Compliance identify issues or gaps? Successful Triple Bottom-Line Compliance programs make it simple for employees to engage, using smart technology to enable them to communicate and contribute to governance.

Voice of Experience

Early in my career, **JIM BODOWITZ,** a mentor and compliance officer at Moody's Investors Services, and previously an executive at several insurance companies and the branch chief for the SEC enforcement division in New York, warned me to be realistic about the risks of blurring the lines between objective gatekeeper and business leader. Blurring those lines makes it difficult to protect the company and the compliance officer. A Compliance program is inadequate if a compliance officer does not act as a gatekeeper. A compliance officer should prepare and commit to a strategy before a crisis hits. Otherwise compliance officers risk being blamed for Compliance issues.

PREPARATION AND STRATEGY VS. REACTION

A mentor once encouraged me to remember to temper my passion for my job with a healthy dose of reality by preparing for potential crises. He warned that if compliance officers do not prepare and commit to a strategy, they could spend too much energy during a crisis avoiding becoming a scapegoat. With the right planning, he joked, the compliance officer will go to lunch while any criminal wrongdoers go to jail. Here are some strategies and tactics to keep you in the lunch line:

STRATEGY	TACTIC
Hone a 360-degree reputation.	• **Build a reputation and network outside your firm.** Join industry committees. Build your own peer group. Build a social media presence as a responsible thought leader. • **Check your gut.** Ask for feedback from your boss and colleagues.
Document your important work.	• **Document every day.** The Circle of Compliance must be documented to show an adequate program. Some legal experts may advise not to document, but carefully consider that doing so may not be in the interests of a compliance officer who is held accountable for mitigating risks. • Personal liability and scapegoating can occur. Carefully documented Compliance efforts go to your *mens rea* and intent to build an effective Triple Bottom-Line program. Documentation shows you are delivering on your duty, even if it isn't perfect.
Manage certain conflicts with an independent advisor.	• **Don't ignore, but manage potential conflicts.** The compliance officer role is inherently conflicted. When a regulatory matter surfaces, remember the inherent conflict between your duties to your employer and the regulators under the laws and regulations. When you struggle to resolve conflicts, you may need to get yourself your own advisor or counsel. You will need a sounding board and a way to make sure your perspective is understood.
Be a gatekeeper for compliance reports and investigations.	• **Carefully consider whether you should interact with regulators when relying on your company's counsel or your own.** When the company's counsel edits your compliance reports and filings, confirm that your gatekeeper role is more prominent than your employment role. If there is an unresolved question, seek independent guidance.

In the Chinese language, the word crisis (危机) is composed of the characters meaning both risk and opportunity. I find that dual meaning has made sense in my own career: a crisis became an opportunity to show regulators, litigants, and the government my company's Sustainable Governance program. By attending depositions as a team that clearly had been working together for years, we were able to help defend a manager. We showed the enforcement attorneys what happened was an unfortunate operational mistake, but not an indication of a systemic failure of business ethics and conduct.

Voice of Experience

BRIAN RUBIN, a partner at Eversheds Sutherland, has extensive experience in securities law on both the prosecution and defense sides. "To effectively defend an enforcement investigation," he says, "it is critical to understand the business, including supervision and Compliance. I find that's impossible to do that without working with a strong compliance officer who can understand—and translate for me and for the regulators—how the business runs. Investigations often focus on one 'bad' aspect of a firm's conduct, but a good compliance officer can help me put that conduct in perspective for the regulators."

Rubin says inappropriate action by one or two employees does not mean a firm's supervisory system was not reasonably designed. "I can't make that argument without a good compliance officer helping me lead the charge and providing me with specific examples of all of the things that the firm did well."

In the aftermath of a crisis, the strength of the compliance officer's network will be on clear display. To offer an extreme example from years ago, a national financial services firm had a rogue sales representative, Joe, who was caught fraudulently taking money from a highly unlikely set of clients. Joe had started stealing from an FBI agent, and through referrals he became the go-to financial advisor for dozens of FBI agents, and he began brazenly stealing from them. Joe was a professional fraudster. He had been caught and kicked out of one state, but was able to move to another state and continue working because technology was less sophisticated then.

When the fraud was finally exposed, the company had to form a SWAT team of senior executives to plan how to deal with the affected FBI agents across the country. Compliance was selected to lead the outreach because Compliance understood the business, had the relationships across various departments, and had a reputation for not just interpreting regulations and protecting the company but also helping it to build a competitive advantage. Compliance officers held forums for the clients to have their accounts and financial plans reviewed, and get assurance they would not lose money and would be more than made whole. Conducting such a forum would have involved gaining admission to a secure federal office building and being ushered into a conference room full of highly agitated, embarrassed, and legally savvy big guys with guns. The compliance officer would have to calm them down, be the face of the company, and mitigate the damage the fraud had done to the firm's credibility. The fraud was resolved without litigation, an outcome that might not have happened if the compliance officers hadn't leveraged a triple bottom-line approach. Most importantly, compliance officers networked with client relationship leaders who helped them prepare to carefully represent the business and its governance before the aggrieved FBI agents.

CHAPTER 5 TAKEAWAY

We have covered networking as a strategy to protect the compliance officer and the organization from crisis risk. Developing a network of Friends of Compliance who engage in mutually beneficial exchanges of information with the compliance officer helps the compliance officer stay diligent, and overall, it leads to more effective controls. That success enhances the personal brand and reputation of the compliance officer, which further promotes networking and Sustainable Governance. The next chapter covers a more specific networking strategy: building legal alliances.

CHAPTER 6

BUILDING ALLIANCES
WITH THE LAWYERS

A frequently misused quotation, "The first thing we do, let's kill all the lawyers," from William Shakespeare's *Henry VI*, isn't about a disdain for lawyers but is homage to their power. The character that utters the line, Dick the Butcher, knows he can't get away with murder if the lawyers are watching.

Compliance work isn't as dramatic as a Shakespearian tragedy, but a true partnership with lawyers, or the lack thereof, can dramatically impact the success of Compliance. If the lawyers agree it's necessary and beneficial to make an impact and build a Sustainable Governance program, not a technical Compliance framework, the compliance officer will be empowered to deliver better results sooner. A compliance officer is more effective if she has a respected and deeply collaborative relationship with the organization's lawyers.

The previous chapter discussed building a network of Friends of Compliance. The legal department can provide the most important and strategic FOCs because of the respect they hold within the organization and the final say they have on certain issues. But a nuance to keep in mind is that attorneys have clients, and compliance officers have Clients, as explained in chapter 4. The perspective of an organization's attorneys on Compliance issues starts off narrower—protecting the client. It's up to the compliance officer to get them on board with Triple Bottom-Line Compliance. Failing to do so can detract from the compliance officer's credibility and ability to deliver productivity and impact.

A compliance officer must think ahead, educate the lawyer, and make a business case for taking a longer-term view rather than just addressing the immediate technical issue.

The following chart shows examples of how counsel is more valuable to the bottom-line business and to mitigating legal risk when it considers the longer-term view.

EXAMPLES OF COMPLIANCE ISSUES	ANSWER TODAY'S TECHNICAL QUESTION	MAKE A LONGER-TERM IMPACT
Public disclosure	• Focus on litigation risk.	• Focus on litigation risk and plain-English descriptions. • Proceed with caution with extra specificity to manage litigation risk without considering regulatory risk, particularly if it is not tailored to commercial realities of operational work flow and demands too much updating or bureaucratic support.
Managing a crisis or investigation	• The lawyers must be loyal to the organization. They cannot represent compliance officers when interests diverge. The attorney-client and work-product privileges belong to the organization.	• Manage appropriately within legal privileges and protections. • Focus on behavioral incentives and cultural impact to avoid scapegoating or fear. • Conduct a sensitive root-cause analysis rewarding accountability and discouraging blaming. • Consider operational and compliance risks with equal weight to legal risks. Consider the benefits of starting to address gaps at issue even before precise legal analysis is complete. • Consider and mitigate conflicts with the organization. • Secure outside advice and protection if needed when interests diverge, and you may be held individually liable by third parties. Remember the legal privileges are the organization's, not the compliance officer's.
Documenting	• Legal privilege is a commonly used tool. Avoid written commentary that can be misunderstood or lead to an inquiry about the working dialogue on compliance issues.	• Legal privilege is narrowly used to protect. • Consider documenting dialogue to show gatekeepers thoughtful grappling with a sensitive Compliance issue and to influence or encourage dialogue when others may prefer to delay resolution.

The compliance officer may have to show Legal that its position on public disclosure is so technical and so protective that it creates risk because Compliance can't operationalize it. When managing a crisis or investigation, the lawyers might warn against putting anything in writing. A compliance officer who aims to not just put out fires but also have sustainable impact will publicly reward cooperative business teams, articulate needed changes and incentivize future behavior. Lawyers may be concerned about documenting or communicating facts and circumstances during an investigation because the understanding of what happened might change over time. But it's hard for Compliance to encourage and communicate cultural expectations that are not written down. Waiting until the end means Compliance loses an opportunity to use a crisis to have an immediate impact.

There's a natural conflict over documentation between Legal trying to protect its clients and Compliance—which has Clients—and needs to show it has been performing its gatekeeper role. Compliance, not the legal team, must worry more about being found negligent by regulators, so compliance officers have more need for documenting an evolving process.

In partnering with the legal team, compliance officers who are not themselves lawyers must strike a balance, showing respect but not blind deference. Compliance officers should think of the lawyers as FOCs, albeit very important FOCs.

Voice of Experience

The late **MARTY LYBECKER** was a partner at prestigious law firms, the chief counsel for the Division of Investment Management at the Securities and Exchange Commission, and an accomplished academic who taught at Duke and Georgetown Universities. As my mentor, he advised me to master the details of the technical compliance requirements to win over skeptical lawyers. A compliance officer must earn credibility by taking the time to do the homework to understand every detail. Early in my career, Lybecker taught me to pause and reread even the most familiar laws, double-checking work and building my credibility.

A compliance officer must be well prepared before approaching an attorney with any kind of issue that they need to collaborate on. Jaynthi Gandhi encourages compliance officers to "demonstrate they are an expert on the business" and the relevant compliance requirements. Compliance officers are typically closer than attorneys to day-to-day operational issues and constraints. They can share this knowledge and, together, compliance officers and attorneys can present unified, cost-effective solutions for the business. If Compliance and legal are aligned and both focused on the Triple Bottom Line, then they're both going to be more influential and a better partner to the business.

"MAKE A CASE" TEMPLATE FOR COMPLIANCE OFFICERS

COMPLIANCE OFFICER STRATEGY	COMPLIANCE OFFICER TACTICS
Tell a story about risk and impact.	**Give a hypothetical example.**
Explain how a legal opinion will increase the lawyer's value as advisor because advice with a long-term vision is more valuable to: 1. The bottom-line business and 2. Mitigating legal risk	Illustrate: 1. How commercial and legal considerations will be addressed. 2. How a sustainable approach decreases systemic risk of confusion and inefficiencies from repeated individual decision making and a case-by-case legal advice approach.

Voice of Experience

BETH SHANKER, the CCO introduced in chapter 2, recommends a joint transparent review by Compliance and Legal of all responses to regulatory inquiries. Collaboration can be formal by establishing a committee, or the stakeholders can simply agree to collaborate to ensure a response is not only technically correct, but it also considers the Compliance and operational impact of statements and promises made.

Lawyers know the laws, rules, and regulations; they may have a blind spot to the importance of regulatory expectations, operational complexities, and a strategy for remediation, if needed. A response to a regulator that doesn't consider all the factors—including the requestor's perceptions and perspective—can bring more risk to an organization. Suppose a lawyer responds to a regulator about a conflict-of-interest process, but the lawyer doesn't understand surveillance, industry norms, or regulatory preferences for mitigation. In this scenario, the lawyer and compliance officer miss opportunities. The lawyer misses a chance to resolve the matter more quickly. The compliance officer misses an opportunity to present the long-term view to help build better mitigation controls and more quickly remediate any gaps.

Collaboration makes solutions more sustainable for the business by avoiding late issue spotting and contradictory advice , particularly when compliance officers are helping the business change or grow. Contradictory advice from Legal and Compliance harms the reputation of both and causes delays. Generally, a business is going to need both Compliance and Legal to say "yes." If one says, "Yes, but ..." that response can be conflicting enough to cause irritation and delay. Throughout corporate America, many debate whether or not Compliance should report to Legal to facilitate coordination, or if they need to be separate because their missions naturally conflict. Either way, a unified response increases productivity and impact.

Jaynthi Gandhi advocates that compliance officers take the initiative when reviewing new product marketing materials to coordinate with Legal if the business hasn't. For example, a compliance officer may review a new digital communications campaign for adherence with regulatory requirements, but the legal implications for intellectual property may be equally important. As the "first line of issue spotting" in many organizations, a compliance officer hasn't delivered for the business if work is delayed because the initial issue spotting is incomplete. The organization should receive a unified, consistent response from the compliance officer and the lawyers—a response that covers all the governance risks.

Legal and Compliance are similar in many ways. Both focus on business ethics and the applicable law, rule, or regulation. In Compliance, there's also a need to document efforts and focus on evolving trends, practices, and preferences that aren't formal law. The spirit and letter of the law can be different. A compliance officer is responsible for both and has multiple loyalties and duties, as discussed in chapter 4.

CHAPTER 6 TAKEAWAY

This chapter covered the importance of compliance officers building an alliance with the lawyers and being well prepared and not too deferential in addressing Compliance issues with Legal. The lawyers represent the client organization and don't have the same gatekeeper role. But collaboration and unified responses from Compliance and Legal can greatly contribute to both an organization's Triple Bottom Line and the compliance officer's credibility and reputation. Compliance officers must get cooperation from a variety of stakeholders, and the next chapter will cover the strategy for mastering the diplomacy involved.

CHAPTER 7

MASTERING DIPLOMACY TO
BUILD SUSTAINABLE INFLUENCE

A compliance officer is making her first big presentation to a conference room full of executives just one month after joining an investment firm. The firm has been through several ethical dust-ups, has had substantial turnover all the way to its top ranks, and is reestablishing its procedures and priorities. The compliance officer has been invited to make a presentation on the potential need to vet conflicts of interest and make sure the personal interests of managers and salespeople do not impair the clients' interests. The successful CEO listens intently to the entire presentation, then surprisingly jumps ahead, asking, "How would you implement within sixty days?"

The compliance officer has anticipated this question and is not about to be left fishing for an answer. She has prepared slides showing three pragmatic options for software systems. She clicks through her deck to show the pros and cons of building versus buying a Compliance system to route employee disclosures for reconciliation against client interests. The CEO requests a single recommendation. After a brief discussion, the executives are on board and the organization is committed to paying for a new system to manage its conflicts.

Winning support for implementing Sustainable Governance solutions is the goal of such a presentation, but it's not always that easy. A compliance officer must be a diplomat, understanding many different stakeholders, and must be someone who doesn't just find problems but fixes them. All the while, the compliance officer should be honing a trust-but-verify brand. The pages ahead cover how to build the relationships and trust that increase a compliance officer's performance, productivity, and influence, delivering a competitive advantage to the organization.

Strong relationships within the business are necessary to win needed technology and influence. Influence is key to the Circle of Compliance, as described in chapter 3, and is key to leading a culture in which engaged employees come to Compliance with issues, without negative stigma, and without having to be prompted or sought out. With Sustainable Governance, Compliance uses its influence to establish a system of cash and non-cash compensation rewards for those who mine for and report inefficiencies and gaps.

When issues are detected and addressed with sustainable solutions, the organization is more productive. A 2017 McKinsey & Co. study titled "Sustainable Compliance: Seven Steps toward Effectiveness and Efficiency," shows a Sustainable Governance program that addresses enterprise-wide material risks and eliminates inefficiencies that can "free up 30 percent of the Compliance function's capacity." Compliance can redirect that 30 percent to proactively work with the business on high impact initiatives. In such an atmosphere, influential compliance officers are trusted advisors *and* business leaders who help improve operational processes, minimize bureaucratic distractions, and strategically incentivize responsible behavior.

TAKE THE TEST

Many successful compliance officers are change agents, business managers, quality assurance representatives, project managers, and therapists as much as they are governance experts. A strategy for mastering these multiple roles is to focus on the *how*, the question asked by the CEO in the story at the beginning of this chapter. How do you fix Compliance issues? Are you a compliance officer who gets temporary, forced results, or one who builds sustainable value and influence? Take the test by answering the following questions:

1. Do you use fear of enforcement or fear of the government when challenged?

2. Do you think what you say is more important than how you say it?

3. Do you think Compliance issues are more important or more serious than business issues?

4. Do you feel as though you are siloed or alone in your work?

5. Do you identify issues that are "out of scope," distancing yourself?

6. When you innovate to support the business, do you exclude business ethics considerations?

If you've answered "yes" to any of these questions, consider whether you are losing an opportunity to be influential and make a more meaningful impact. **Compliance officers tend to focus too much on the ends rather than the means. To build influence, focus on the means.**

MEANS: LOSE THE HAMMER

MEANS	END
Engagement Smile and slow down to get others involved, regardless of the deadlines, risks, and time pressure. Avoid perceived lectures or mandates.	*Protection* Guard the organization and your reputation.
Collaboration A compliance officer is more than an individual contributor. Collaboration is key to identifying the most germane governance issues and solutions.	*Sustainable Impact* Minimize bureaucracy.
Pragmatic Support Give shoulder-to-shoulder support to the business. They know the risks. You'll be better educated about business challenges, opportunities, products, and target customers.	*Organization buy-in and FOCs* They accept your advice as their own best idea. See chapter 5.
Sustainable Governance Use best practices and business ethics. Be precise and transparent on what is required and what is risky because it raises an ethical issue.	*Compliance Culture* Leave a mark beyond responding to a technical issue in the moment.

Building influence takes time. A fantastic place for compliance officers to start is with building trust by excelling as a project manager, tailoring surveillance to material business risks, and connecting with Glients. Compliance officers should not assume that trust comes automatically with their job title or that they do not need to show trust in others. An influential compliance officer makes an impact by earning the trust of the business while maintaining his gatekeeper role. Trust is earned as the compliance officer shows knowledge of the regulatory landscape, listens to colleagues, and develops approaches that meet current and future commercial or organizational needs.

"He who does not trust enough, will not be trusted."

—LAO TZU

Voice of Experience

LARRY BLOCK, the CCO introduced in chapter 4, encourages compliance officers to build rapport throughout the Compliance cycle. For example, instead of viewing training and outreach as just educational, they can take it as an important opportunity to build rapport and trust. Compliance officers should design training so that they can learn from their clients and build relationships.

When clients have issues to report and questions to ask, they're less likely to be intimidated or hesitant to call a compliance officer they have come to know during training and outreach. Block encourages compliance officers to get out of their offices and travel if necessary to make the outreach and training face-to-face. "People can start to get to know you, and see that you are engaged and that you are there for them, even before there is a problem."

Compliance officers lose an opportunity to build relationships and trust if they rely solely on e-training or buy off-the-shelf training that has not been customized for their organization. Presenting training that is relevant, smart, and tailored builds rapport.

Voices of Experience

Some compliance officers aspire to be brought into business projects early on, but **MARYJEAN BONADONNA**, CCO at AXA Advisors, believes in a more integrated approach: "Compliance has to be embedded—not just inserted." An influential compliance officer doesn't just talk to the business about legal requirements. The compliance officer engages on non-compliance issues too—business products, internal controls, or whatever the team is focusing on.

Bonadonna invokes a folk tale about people contributing ingredients for a stranger's soup to describe the collaboration she encourages: "You don't need an invitation to the table." It's just assumed you will be there. You are there "flavoring the Stone Soup with spices" or whatever needs to be done to build a relationship so strong that the compliance officer is the go-to person during a crisis.

Businesses are looking for all employees, not just the business teams, to be aligned with their core values and goals. **KAT OLIN**, CCO at Indus Capital Partners, LLC, encourages compliance officers to show pride in, and add value to, their organization by participating in marketing efforts, making business referrals, spearheading successful initiatives, and sharing data that can be leveraged to help grow the business. A compliance officer can be objective and independent and still introduce certain business partners or prospects to the organization, helping to build its credibility, brand, and sales pipeline. Compliance officers build rapport and trust by showing they are there to help even when there isn't a problem.

External networking with peers at other organizations allows compliance officers not only to stay current with industry best practices, but also to enhance their own careers by tapping into successful initiatives that others have adopted. By proactively networking outside an organization, a compliance officer can build relationships that show Compliance—traditionally viewed as an expense center—is thinking outside the box and looking for additional ways to add value.

TEN WAYS TO ADD VALUE

Compliance officers often use a matrix to assess various levels of risk, creating a visual tool to manage their priorities. Why not also have a matrix showing how the compliance officer adds value to a business? What follows are ten contributions that can be used in a matrix chart to record the added value, designate its priority, level of compliance involvement, and future opportunities. A compliance officer could track how Compliance delivered on any or all of the ten items throughout the year, and then show it to the business to build trust and rapport. The ten contributions represent a combination of protection, productivity, and impact.

VALUE CATEGORY	PRIORITY TO BUSINESS—H/M/L
1. Support prospective client and investor due diligence.	
2. Apply on behalf of the organization for financial grants and incentives that require good governance. Compliance can design a program to ensure the organization meets the requirements. Bringing in extra money is a clear, measurable way to add value.	
3. Help launch new products.	
4. Leverage analytical and research skills for certain business projects. A compliance officer can analyze regulations and rules, which can help the business figure out whether to make an acquisition, for example.	
5. Find process improvements and fix errors before they grow.	
6. Be a warehouse for data, books, and records.	
7. Manage regulatory relationships and advocate change as needed.	
8. Increase client engagement and protect the brand.	
9. Develop expertise and influence industry developments, regulatory developments, and product innovation through benchmarking.	
10. Fuel employee recruitment and retention through engagement. Examples: trust and integrity leadership awards for departments, spot bonuses for finding gaps.	

LEVEL OF HELP FROM COMPLIANCE— H/M/L	METRICS FROM REPORTING— COUNT AND TRACK SPECIFIC EXAMPLES	OPPORTUNITIES TO DO MORE—Y/N

THREE WAYS TO CHANGE AN ORGANIZATION'S DYNAMIC

Some compliance officers may be reticent to start using a value matrix or try other new ways to build trust and rapport because they've been around the organization too long. But it is never too late to start, even if there is an adversarial dynamic in the organization. A compliance officer can try these three ways to change the dynamic:

1. Invite someone from the business to speak at a Compliance staff meeting about "What Compliance does well and what can be done better."

2. Make it clear that employees will be rewarded for helping and being cooperative. Partner with Human Resources to change how employee performance is calculated, and include a Compliance grade for identifying and reporting issues, helping implement policies, and responding in timely ways to requests for needs, such as certification or training.

3. Give credit during audits to the business for cooperation such as self-reporting and expediting surveillance and testing.

Influencers are people who get things done. A compliance officer who can manage and master a project plan so the work is high quality and on time will earn influence. As discussed in chapter 4, just having a plan makes almost any issue manageable, and improves the compliance officer's ability to communicate with and engage others and track progress. Now comes the question of whether the project management process is as important as the results.

In the story that began this chapter, the well-prepared compliance officer who had three options ready to present for a technology solution was asked to recommend one option and did so. Now suppose she is in a different situation where she presents three alternative solutions to the question of how the company can show it is giving the customer the best price and valuation. The people in the room are looking for a specific rule to follow defining "best." She explains there is guidance, but not a specific rule or law defining the term. Someone flippantly says, "You haven't a clue about the requirements." The executives are critical or disappointed because they fear that without a rule they are giving the compliance officer too much discretion.

Remembering chapter 4 of this book, the compliance officer realizes her preparation should have included assessing whether she is working with Rule Followers, Rule Benders, or Rule Breakers. Dealing with resistance is part of the job. Adding value in the face of resistance requires preparation and knowing the audience. So, the rule for the compliance officer is, "Know thy client." **Heather Traeger,** CCO at Teacher Retirement System of Texas, reminds compliance officers "to listen first, before you do anything." Compliance officers can build a sustainable program if they listen, adjust to their audience, and avoid any perception they are bulldozing through an organization.

The following chart shows some types of resistance a compliance officer might encounter from Glients, and some tactical responses.

RESISTANCE	RESPONSE
State requirements are too prescriptive.	• Determine if you're working with Rule Followers, Breakers, or Benders. • Be calm and flexible, adapt as needed. • Cite benchmarking, including others who are complying, risks of not complying, ways to achieve another business objective with the same process.
States requirements are not clear enough.	• Determine if you're working with Rule Followers, Breakers, or Benders. • Be calm and focus on a clear, concise message. • Cite the principle-based rule, and cover benefits of tailoring governance, such as discretion, to use business judgment.
They want you to make the final decision.	• Give multiple options, then give a recommendation.
They don't want you to make the final decision; they want to reserve authority.	• Give multiple options. • Have a recommendation ready in case you are asked. • Proceed cautiously with clear research of pros and cons for each option.

Voices of Experience

One of my first bosses, **RICHARD SILVER**, the then general counsel at AXA Financial, taught me that you'll know you have made a long-lasting impact when you hear someone else articulate your advice as their own. He explained to me that an influential compliance officer doesn't need credit. Rather, the compliance officer needs to be part of the organization's governance and serve as "quality assurance."

CHAPTER 7 TAKEAWAY

In this chapter, we've covered strategies for forming relationships and building trust to be influential. These strategies include being prepared, having a plan, knowing the audience, and focusing on the means and not just the ends. We offered a self-assessment for compliance officers to discover whether they are missing opportunities to be influential. To achieve Triple Bottom-Line Compliance, a compliance officer must earn trust and be seen as helpful to the organization beyond just finding Compliance gaps. Compliance officers are influential when they think beyond the crisis at hand and propose sustainable solutions they know the organization can embrace because they have gotten to know the people and built rapport. When the inevitable crises occur, the organization will look to the compliance officer for leadership and guidance. At that point, the compliance officer must fall back on his or her ethical True North, which is the subject of the next chapter.

CHAPTER 8
BEING YOUR TRUE NORTH
IN ETHICAL CONFLICTS

*"Power is not revealed by striking hard or often, but
by striking true."*

—HONORÉ DE BALZAC

t's the time of year when Compliance departments are busy preparing
the annual certifications that must be filed with government regulators to disclose compliance gaps. Several staff members are conducting
research, scheduling interviews, and obtaining supporting certifications
at the fictional firm I'll call Go South Investments. Typically, the most
senior Compliance person signs the certification for the good health of the
entire Compliance program, and at Go South that person is the CCO.
When the deadline day comes, the new head of Compliance, who has
been at the company for three months, surprises a junior compliance
officer, who has been at the company for more than five years by bringing
him the annual certification and telling him to sign it. The compliance
officer is in a quandary because he doesn't know if the enterprise-wide
due diligence has been completed, and he doesn't think it is his role to

sign the certification. But he is told that if he doesn't sign, Go South will be in breach of legal requirements, and the regulators are going to be upset. Worried about his job, the young compliance officer signs the certification.

Compliance officers may rarely face such stark dilemmas, but at times there are conflicts between responsibility to the organization and the gatekeeper function for government regulators. In our story, Compliance management at Go South was not being true to its Clients, as described throughout this book. Compliance officers need to balance the need to be client-centric and effective gatekeepers, equally guarding the employer's interests and delivering on legal requirements. In this case, Compliance must give regulators a genuine and accurate certification of good health. If a gap were to be discovered later, but mistakenly not disclosed in the certification, the firm and the unprepared compliance officer both could have been held accountable for being negligent.

Compliance officers, to make an impact, must be aligned with and believe in the culture, the organization, and the business efforts they serve. Not surprisingly, it's rare to see a compliance officer job description without "strong ethics needed" under qualifications. The term "True North Ethics" means more than it appears at first; it means there is an authentic fit for a compliance officer within an organization. They have a similar mindset for governance and a compliance officer's gatekeeper role. Without that alignment, a compliance officer may be too focused on protection only and may struggle to be a beacon for the rest of the organization on how to deploy good business ethics when facing conflicts of interests.

PROTECTION STRATEGY	GATEKEEPER APPROACH FOR GLIENT	CLIENT IMPACT
Bare minimum compliance	Underactive gatekeeper role	Narrow engagement
Hard-line compliance	Overactive gatekeeper role	Issues edicts to the business

Essentially, a compliance officer may take a hard line or revert to bare minimum compliance to protect his career and reputation. When employing this survival mode tactic, compliance officers let the business decide whether to take risks. They keep their head down, trying to avoid personal liability. If you have read this far in this book, you know that compliance officers should be helping to identify and mitigate risks and adding value with efficiencies and making an impact, while still protecting themselves and the organizations.

After compliance officers are aligned with their True North Ethics, they should turn to managing their reputation as a beacon of values and culture for the rest of the organization. In a difficult situation like the one described at the beginning of this chapter, True North Ethics will be tested but an aligned compliance officer will more easily carry out the gatekeeper role. There is no one True North because it varies by an individual compliance officer's personal priorities and by the values of the organization. Certain social and behavioral norms are expected, but there are cultural differences and varying facts and nuanced circumstances around the fringes where people can reasonably disagree about what action is ethical. Compliance officers are encouraged to be self-aware about their own preferences. As discussed in chapter 2, compliance officers must perform due diligence when they find and take a job to make sure there's a fit from a cultural and governance perspective.

Being a True North beacon doesn't mean that a compliance officer should preach personal standards or project a sense of being more ethical than others. The alignment is more subtle than that. The behavioral incentives discussed earlier in the book are about fostering alignment, not about creating a visible bully pulpit. Ethics are personal, and talking about them can come off as preachy. But behind the gatekeeper role, there is real enforcement power. To garner the C-suite credibility and executive presence they need, compliance officers should be true to their ethics without having too much ego involved. An arrogant or myopic compliance officer will have trouble managing conflicts especially in nuanced situations.

Voice of Experience

THE CCO at a large mutual fund complex on the West Coast compared being a compliance officer to walking a tightrope. A successful compliance officer conveys confidence, composure, and calmness while under pressure. Encountering a compliance issue while operating simultaneously as a gatekeeper and a client-centric advisor requires balance and responsiveness. Compliance officers should be energetic and positive, but should also remember they are solving a problem and shouldn't get too excited about the challenge.

For example, if a compliance officer hears about a potential bribery claim, and appears too excited at the prospect of leading an interesting investigation, it will appear as though the compliance officer is focused more on ego than on helping the organization. Likewise, to earn credibility, particularly when providing advice, a compliance officer must balance listening, getting business buy-in, and adjusting to the business needs on the one hand with independence, objectivity, and decisiveness. And it's not easy to keep that composure, particularly in tough situations where the compliance officer is focused on being a gatekeeper. Striking that balance is important to build influence as well as ensure the compliance officer is aligned with his True North Ethics.

CHALLENGE YOUR MOXIE

The following three case studies explain how a Sustainable Governance approach will prepare a compliance officer with a good response, not just a reaction. Read each as if you are the compliance officer and note how you would handle the scenario.

1. You are asked to sign the auditors' management representation letter. You're a pleaser, you like to get things done, and this is your job as compliance officer. You read the letter. The auditors ask you if you know about any fraud or gaps in internal controls. They need a signature today, but you realize you didn't ask for any supporting certifications, you have not had a discussion with any lawyers, and you wonder whether you, as a gatekeeper, should sign a "management" letter.

2. You just completed a challenging and rewarding year of Compliance. You've struggled, but your Annual Compliance Report is finished and ready to go. You'll send it to the business to help them remember your value add, and to the regulators, prospective clients, and investors to show you confirmed the effectiveness of the Compliance program. Compliance is a continuous cycle (chapter 3). You know there's always an active matter to manage. Not having one would be a warning sign you are avoiding digging in and helping out. You want to be transparent about issues found and not yet fully remediated.

3. You find yourself on the other side of your boss's mahogany desk on a conference call with outside counsel. The words are carefully parsed, but the message is clear, your report is too transparent. They advocate deleting all active matters including any high-level descriptions. They explain, "Facts about open matters will change throughout the year."

4. Your company receives a regulatory inquiry about a major data breach and its cybersecurity program. The regulator's enforcement department is on the case and penalties seem certain. This is more investigation than a routine inquiry. Outside lawyers are engaged and a carefully written response is underway. You expected it. You were on top of the issue. You found customer data wasn't protected as needed and you reported it.

5. Nonetheless, you find yourself in a windowless conference room, with free food and drinks, as a partner at a well-respected law firm starts to ask you questions, weaving a story you quickly realize entails you as a target:

6. "Walk me through what you meant with this email. I'm confused."

7. "Are you sure you clearly briefed and communicated the issue?"

8. "You knew the organization wasn't following legal requirements and clients were at risk and you didn't do anything else?"

For each of these scenarios, you are in a strong position if you carefully selected your employer (chapter 2) and protected your brand (chapter 5). After you take a deep breath and confirm your perceptions and facts, carefully consider your next step and whether it is aligned with your True North Ethics and obligations as a gatekeeper.

The following chart summarizes the respective quandaries presented in the case studies above and suggests a response for each.

QUANDARY	RESPONSE	TACTICS
1. Do you sign?	Yes—consult and edit the letter.	Ask to consult with the organization's attorney, understand the breadth of your affirmation, and edit the text to fit your role and the facts. Consider a sustainable alternative to establish a disclosure committee of cross-functional stakeholders to meet, discuss, and possibly gather supporting certifications before execution of any affirmation.
2. Do you object?	Yes—ask "why" and seek transparency.	Confirm with multiple advisors your disclosures are accurate and use your skills (chapter 6) to educate the lawyers about disadvantages of an orientation focused on potential legal risks at the expense of transparency.
3. Do you cooperate?	Yes—manage conflicts with your own advisor and rely on your focs (chapter 5).	Continue to collaborate, with the assistance of your own advisor, and confirm you have Directors & Officers insurance. Get counsel if you need it. The earlier, the better. Once statements are made to the government, contradicting those statements is complicated.

Voice of Experience

HEATHER TRAEGER, the CCO introduced in the previous chapter, explains the benefits of not succumbing to pressure to give an immediate answer to Compliance questions, especially those involving tough ethical issues. Most situations do not require a snap decision. She encourages compliance officers to carefully handle situations with a response that shows that the compliance officer is listening. For example: "I hear your question and I understand what you are asking. I will do the research and get back to you in the morning." The specific time frame shows commitment to provide an answer, which should be not only technically appropriate but also aligned with the compliance officer's True North Ethics.

Taking time to be prepared, a compliance officer can leverage challenging situations to advocate Sustainable Governance and, in the process, manage personal liability. A compliance officer can show leadership as a beacon for others facing ethical quandaries by helping set and communicate the organization's values and ethical standards. A compliance officer should encourage others to respond, not react, by applying lessons learned through behavioral economics. This brings us back to a point made near the beginning of this book: understanding behavioral drivers and incentivizing behavior is more effective than dictating rules and expecting adherence because Compliance publishes an edict. Communicating True North Ethics, the compliance officer shows employees two things: (1) their behavior matters; if they don't comply, others will be harmed, and (2) within the organization, social norms and business judgments are shared. Values and good ethics are expected.

A compliance officer avoids bureaucracy and predictable surprises if he or she can build a culture that encourages engagement with Compliance, where self-reporting to Compliance is valued and rewarded as a form of leadership. Compliance issues can be addressed more easily if resolved early and continuously with employee feedback.

As for managing personal liability, consider the case of Tonawanda

Coke Corporation. The Buffalo, New York, area company and its environmental manager were held accountable by the Department of Justice in 2014 for violations of environmental laws, including eleven counts for violating the Clean Air Act and three counts for violating the Resource Conservation and Recovery Act. The company paid millions in fines, and the executive was sentenced to prison. The executive knew the company was polluting, allowed it to continue, and hid the violations from government regulators. The government's case was based on the concept that he believed no one would be harmed, so he rationalized there would be no victims, and that is why he failed to adhere to his duty to either remedy or report the violations. A compliance officer can prevent such a dire outcome by sending a message of expected conduct and showing the value of self-reporting.

An example of a culture of responsible Compliance is Ketchum, Idaho, a city that worked for years to reduce light pollution in the night sky. The city achieved designation as a Dark Sky Reserve after adopting an ordinance restricting lighting. Remarkably, none of the residents has had to be ticketed for noncompliance. They understand adhering to the ordinance is in their city's interest, because it will benefit the local economy with increased tourism and jobs.

SIGNS OF TRUE NORTH ETHICS

Examples of seeking compliance by sending messages about values and good behavior are all around us. The more effective messages drive better behavior by using a carrot, instead of a hammer, and personalize any harm. Instead of a public garden sign saying, "Curb your dog," the sign says. "Please respect our plantings." A residential street sign that says, "We love our children, 20 MPH," is more impactful than simply "Speed Limit 20 MPH."

For ethics hotline reporting of suspicious activities, many compliance officers borrow from the government's campaign against terrorism: "If you see something, say something." Communication campaigns help build a culture of responsibility and values. Messages directing employees to use an ethics hotline are less likely to get a response unless they are part of a Triple Bottom-Line Compliance program with behavioral incentives and a defense to negative reporting stigma. A program to increase employee engagement should illustrate the direct impact of unethical behavior and give carrots, or rewards, to leaders who find and report compliance issues. Compliance officers educate employees about their direct impact on others, with statements such as, "Your integrity, our integrity," or, "Help us protect our jobs and reputation."

Training helps build a culture and set ethical norms and organizational values. Many companies require employees to complete annual training about how to comply with laws, rules, and regulations, but employees struggle to pay attention and relate to such bare technical material. Triple Bottom-Line Compliance training addresses the rationalizations that lead to poor business judgment and noncompliance. Training is used as outreach to drive behavior into alignment with values. Compliance officers use technology and efficiently present case studies, hypotheticals, and real examples of employee rewards for finding and reporting inefficiencies and compliance gaps; implications of noncompliance, linking employee behavior directly to harm and disproving rationalizations that noncompliance isn't hurting anyone; and employees adhering to ethical norms, debunking rationalizations that ignoring compliance is the social norm.

Triple Bottom-Line training reinforces social norms as to what is acceptable. It encourages a self-reporting culture and provides immediate incentives and rewards for such reporting. The training doesn't just focus on Rule Breakers, but offers scenarios in which many employees are following the rules, countering the "everybody does it" rationalization for misbehavior.

CHAPTER 8 TAKEAWAY

This chapter has covered the challenging situations that result from compliance officers' responsibility to protect their organizations and serve as a gatekeeper for government regulators. To avoid focusing only on the protection, compliance officers must be aligned and believe in the culture, the organizations, and the business efforts they serve. This alignment creates a True North ethical beacon that compliance officers can communicate and use to advocate for Sustainable Governance while managing their personal liability. The personal brand and legacy that compliance officers bring to their role is the subject of the next chapter.

CHAPTER 9

CONTRIBUTE A LEGACY!
BRAND YOURSELF

During 2005, the first full year that many financial services companies were required to have a CCO, the business press glamorized the role, as though CCOs were industry rock stars sipping champagne in fancy restaurants. I remember some of us gathered a pile of rocks. Each drew a simple black star on a rock with a Sharpie to have as a paperweight on our desks and remind us how difficult it is to understand our role unless you live it.

Then and now, compliance officers spend their time in the trenches, where many are trying to build sustainable programs when the status quo is to treat compliance as a cost center. People looking in from outside—such as the consultants, outside counsels, and auditors we work with—tend to miss the complexity of building a program that makes a compliance officer's contribution more sustainable and enjoyable. But compliance officers who achieve Sustainable Governance are collectively creating new norms and perceptions for the profession. Most notably, they are achieving ROI.

Compliance has a reputation for being reactive and reflective. Compliance officers should consider rebranding their departments, systems, or programs to convey the new Triple Bottom-Line Compliance concepts discussed in this book. The goal should be to show that Compliance is a core value for the organization, that its programs and systems are there to help incentivize behavior that's aligned with the core culture.

WHAT'S IN A NAME?

If you were creating a Compliance department from scratch and could give it any branding, what name would you choose? If you agree that Compliance sounds too barebones, jot your ideas in the blanks below:

Business Interests and Integrity	Governance, Ethics, and Integrity
Business Principles	_____
Value and Culture	_____
Corporate Behavior	_____

A popular brand of Compliance is heavily associated with protection, sometimes carried out in a bureaucratic way. If a compliance officer adopts all the strategies in this book and creates a system of Sustainable Governance, it may also be time to retire the name Compliance and adopt branding that connotes the value-add. People in the profession have been talking about such a rebranding but it has not caught on yet.

Compliance officers are not rock stars, but they can be perceived as senior leaders who are collaborative, build trusting relationships, and leave a legacy of Triple Bottom-Line Compliance. This reconceptualization of the role is grounded in research. An influential Harvard Business Review article in February 2007 titled "In Praise of the Incomplete Leader," knocked down the idea of leaders as flawless visionaries with all the skills needed to make and implement big decisions by edict. Authors Deborah Ancona, Thomas W. Malone, Wanda J. Orlikowski, and Peter M. Senge supported the concept that strong skills in building relationships, and sense making, or collaboration can make one an effective leader.

Compliance has traditionally rested on the notions that leaders issue edicts, that people will follow a decisive leader, and that money is the primary motivator of employee behavior. **A compliance officer must act like a leader and be perceived as a leader—they must build relationships with FOCs, lawyers, and regulators to deliver Triple Bottom-Line Compliance.** Studies show people don't always follow edicts and, as discussed in chapters 1 and 8, behavioral economics has provided a model for a more collaborative, relationship-based motivation for employees engaging with Compliance. It won't be easy. Compliance Officers need to master a careful balance of opposing perspectives. The term Glient captures the need to strike a balance in those relationships between being client-centric and being a gatekeeper. A strong compliance officer is clear, definitive, and decisive but only after listening, collaborating, and explaining why a regulatory requirement is, for instance, a hard and fast rule that needs to be adhered to.

If conflict occurs—for example if there is disagreement among Rule Followers, Rule Benders, and Rule Breakers—it doesn't mean that a compliance officer is not being a leader. Conflict is inherent in the role of the compliance officer, and it's part of the lives of all leaders.

To explain how a compliance officer creates value by improving policies, consider this scenario: *A new head of Compliance comes in hoping to hit the ground running. She examines her predecessor's annual compliance report and immediately notices the compliance officer forgot to cover new anti-fraud best practices. In fact, the policies look as though they haven't been updated for a few years. A natural reaction might be to complain to the new boss to show the baseline from which the compliance officer will be making improvements. The compliance officer should keep in mind that the organization is watching how she leads, and that she too will have a successor someday. She is not going to create value by criticizing others. Compliance officers should continue to perpetuate a strong, supportive community that gets the best work done under the circumstances.*

Heather Traeger, the Texas CCO, explains that a slight change in vocabulary can promote a collective, instead of competitive, community of compliance officers. For example, compliance officers can respect the work of a predecessor by "building on" his foundation, not "improving" it. With a collective focus on strategy and Sustainable Governance, compliance programs will get smarter in how they protect organizations, markets, and customers.

An annual compliance report—a required certification in some industries—provides an important opportunity for compliance officers to present a business case for their value-add. They can adopt the Triple Bottom-Line approach and explain how they protected the organization, adhered to the requirements, but also delivered an ROI and productive impact on the business.

ROI examples include:

- **Protection:** Compliance identifies enterprise risks earlier, keeps pace with regulatory expectations for analyzing data, and identifies risks more systemically.

- **Productivity:** Compliance spends less time gathering and submitting data because it has implemented smart technology. That data is collected not just for the regulators but is shared and leveraged with the business. Compliance assesses and spends resources on material business risks and identifies inefficiencies.

- **Impact:** Compliance increases engagement from all the stakeholders by involving all departments in addressing compliance issues and producing the information flow necessary for the annual compliance report. The annual report provides information the business can leverage for its own planning.

This chapter has covered how compliance officers who believe in Sustainable Governance are collectively creating new norms and perceptions for the profession. They can and should reflect that legacy when they brand themselves as leaders and report on their work.

As Andrew Parry so eloquently stated in the foreword of this book, the message of *Triple Bottom-Line Compliance* is indeed timely in this transitioning world. Strong compliance creates a healthy culture for businesses to thrive and adapt. Mastering the challenges to deliver begins today, one compliance officer at a time.

Triple bottom-line compliance is absolutely key to creating resilient, productive, and sustainable businesses that offer a competitive advantage. This approach is timeless if integrated at all business levels, and especially if it's reinforced by continuing education as I've shared in the content of this book.

END OF BOOK TAKEAWAY

So how do you take the methodologies and strategies you've acquired here and motivate yourself to make an impact that not only elevates your organization but also your reputation and your career? Start by rebranding the effort at your own organization. Don't just practice your new strategies—share them. Get involved in outside compliance organizations and industry groups to continue the conversation. Manage the imbalance of relying on technical experience without a strategic, sustainable focus. Share lessons with your colleagues and peers and expand your education by participating in professional conferences to remain current in the field. Above all, always build toward making a sustainable impact.

RESOURCES AND FURTHER READING

COMPLIANCE PROGRAMS

U.S. government and regulatory websites:

www.sec.gov/rules/final/ia-2204.htm

www.sec.gov/rules/final/ia-2256.htm

www.sec.gov/info/cco/adviser_compliance_questions.htm

www.finra.org/sites/default/files/Industry/p016464.pdf

www.nfa.futures.org

www.justice.gov/criminal-fraud/page/file/937501/download

BEHAVIORAL ECONOMICS

Ariely, Dan. "Our Buggy Moral Code." Filmed February 2009 in Long Beach, CA. TED video, 16:14. https://www.ted.com/talks/dan_ariely_on_our_buggy_moral_code.

Flemming, John H., and James K. Harter. "The Next Discipline: Applying Behavioral Economics to Drive Growth & Profitability." Gallup. (September 22, 2012).

Incentive Research Foundation. "How to Effectively Harness Behavioral Economics to Drive Employee Performance and Engagement." Market Research. April 26, 2017. http://theirf.org/research/how-to-effectively-harness-behavioral-economics-to-drive-employee-performance-and-engagement/2072.

Mazar, Nina, and Dan Ariely. "Dishonesty in Everyday Life and Its Policy Implications." *American Marketing Association 25, no. 1 (2006).*

SOCIAL EXCHANGE STUDY
Saks, Alan M. "Antecedents and Consequences of Employee Engagement." *Journal of Managerial Psychology* 21. no. 7 (2006): 600-619.

COMPLIANCE OFFICER LIABILITY
www.sec.gov/news/statement/supporting-role-of-chief-compliance-officers.html

Kaminski, Piotr, Daniel Mikkelsen, Thomas Poppensieker, and Kate Robu. "Sustainable Compliance: Seven Steps toward Effectiveness and Efficiency." McKinsey & Company. (February 2017): https://www.mckinsey.com/business-functions/risk/our-insights/sustainable-compliance-seven-steps-toward-effectiveness-and-efficiency.

FINTECH
Manyika, James, Michael Chui, Mehdi Miremadi, Jacques Bughin, Katy George, Paul Willmont, and Martin Dewhurst. "A Future that Works: Automation, Employment, and Productivity." McKinsey & Company. McKinsey Global Institute. (January 2017).

PRINCIPLES FOR RESPONSIBLE INVESTMENT
United Nations website:
www.unpri.org/about

TONAWANDA COKE CASE

The US Department of Justice. "Tonawanda Coke and Manager Sentenced for Violating the Clean Air Act and Resource Conservation and Recovery Act." Office of Public Affairs. March 19, 2014. https://www.justice.gov/opa/pr/tonawanda-coke-and-manager-sentenced-violating-clean-air-act-and-resource-conservation-and.

APPENDIX
DUE DILIGENCE CHART

DUE DILIGENCE LIST
1. How long was the last compliance officer there? Why did he or she leave?
2. Go to your network for informal feedback on culture. Is the culture collaborative or is it command and control?
3. Is employee engagement welcome or is transparency on a need-to-know basis?
4. Ask about and look for indication of ethics as a core value and tone at the top. Is the culture aligned with your True North Ethics? See chapter 8.
5. Is there D&O insurance for your role?
6. When reporting line independence and protection, consider your personal Business Continuity Plan (BCP) for your reputation and your brand. For senior roles, reporting to an independent board is optimal.
7. Is there collaboration with the legal department or access to legal resources?
8. When was last audit or exam? What is biggest risk?
9. Consider who are Friends of Compliance (FOCs). See chapter 5.
10. How is the business health?
11. What is the percentage of Rule Followers, Rule Benders, and Rule Breakers? See chapter 4.

PROS	CONS